Breakfast in Bed

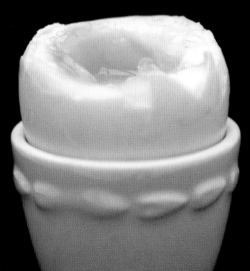

For my friends – absent, old and new – and
for Smudge, whose capacity for both joy
and scrambled eggs is boundless

Breakfast in Bed

Laura James

Absolute Press

Breakfast in Bed

First published in Great Britain in 2009 by Absolute Press
Scarborough House, 29 James Street West, Bath, England BA1 2BT
Phone: 44 (0) 1225 316013 Fax: 44 (0) 1225 445836
E-mail: info@absolutepress.co.uk / Online: www.absolutepress.co.uk

For Absolute Press
Publisher: Jon Croft
Commissioning Editor: Meg Avent
Editorial Assistant: Andrea O'Connor
Art Director: Matt Inwood

Recipe photography by Lisa Barber / Food styling by Trish Hilferty

Duck Egg, p2 Duck Egg with Asparagus, p3 Banana Bread, p6 Chocolate Fondue, p6 Croissants, p26 The Full Works, p31
Pancakes with Maple Syrup, p37 Blueberry Scones, p41 Teacup, p52 Duck Egg with Asparagus, p55 Strawberry, p64
Bellinis, p67 Pigs in Blankets, p81 Turtle Pancakes, pp82-83 Smoked Haddock Soup, p103 Arancini, p107
Banana Bread, p117 Scallops in Garlic and Parsley Butter, p126 Chocolate Fondue, p135 Blueberry Scones, p158

All other photography by Tim James at The Gray Gallery

ISBN-13: 9781906650001
Printed and bound in Italy by L.E.G.O. S.p.A. Vicenza

Under the covers

Glossary of American terms

An explanation for American readers of some of the culinary terms used in Breakfast in Bed

Ingredients

bacon rasher bacon slice

bicarbonate of soda baking soda

caster sugar superfine sugar

celery stick celery stalk

coriander (fresh) cilantro

dark chocolate bittersweet chocolate

dark muscovado sugar soft dark brown sugar

double cream heavy cream

easy-blend dried yeast rapid/instant dried yeast

eggs extra large eggs

flaked almonds sliced almonds

full-fat milk whole milk

golden syrup light corn syrup

icing sugar powdered sugar

kippers smoked herring

knob of butter stick of butter

milk chocolate semisweet chocolate

plain flour all-purpose flour

prawn shrimp

red pepper red bell pepper

self-raising flour self-rising flour

single cream light cream

spring onion green onion

stock broth/stock

strong white flour bread flour

swede turnip/rutabaga

Tabasco sauce hot pepper sauce

unsalted butter sweet butter

vanilla pod vanilla bean

Equipment

cake tin cake pan

loaf tin loaf pan

baking parchment parchment paper

baking sheet cookie sheet

baking tin/tray baking pan

roasting tin roasting pan

greaseproof paper parchment paper

frying pan skillet

grilled broiled

8

Weight

7g	$^1/_4$ oz
20g	$^3/_4$ oz
25-30g	1 oz
40g	$1^1/_2$ oz
50g	$1^3/_4$ oz
60-65g	$2^1/_4$ oz
70-75g	$2^1/_2$ oz
80g	$2^3/_4$ oz
90g	$3^1/_4$ oz
100g	$3^1/_2$ oz
110-115g	4 oz
120-130g	$4^1/_2$ oz
140g	5 oz
150g	$5^1/_2$ oz
175-180g	6 oz
200g	7 oz
220-225g	8 oz
250-260g	9 oz
300g	$10^1/_2$ oz
325g	$11^1/_2$ oz
350g	12 oz
400g	14 oz
450g	1 pound
500g	1 pound 2 oz
1kg	$2^1/_4$ pounds
2kg	$4^1/_2$ pounds

Volume

50ml	$1^3/_4$ fl oz
60ml	2 fl oz (4 tablespoons/$^1/_4$ cup)
75ml	$2^1/_2$ fl oz (5 tablespoons)
90ml	3 fl oz ($^3/_8$ cup)
100ml	$3^1/_2$ fl oz
125ml	4 fl oz ($^1/_2$ cup)
150ml	5 fl oz ($^2/_3$ cup)
175ml	6 fl oz
200ml	7 fl oz
250ml	8 fl oz (1 cup)
500ml	18 fl oz
1 litre	35 fl oz (4 cups)

Length

5mm	$^1/_4$ inch
1cm	$^1/_2$ inch
2cm	$^3/_4$ inch
2.5cm	1 inch
3cm	$1^1/_4$ inches
4cm	$1^1/_2$ inches
6cm	$2^1/_2$ inches
8cm	$3^1/_4$ inches
10cm	4 inches
20cm	8 inches
40cm	16 inches

I'VE ALWAYS BEEN rather envious of the heroines in Victorian novels who, deciding life was just all too much, simply took to their beds. With four children, two dogs, two cats and work to do, sadly I can't manage months on end under the covers, but I have to admit that I do spend as much time as possible tucked up under my duvet.

Eating in bed is thrilling. There's a frisson of decadence about it, even if you're only munching toast and Marmite. We seem to live life at a hundred miles per hour, so time lazily spent feels like the height of luxury.

The best way to eat in bed is definitely with someone you love. It can be deeply romantic with champagne and fripperies, fun or simply cosy. Munching bacon sandwiches together, huddled up against the cold, is a bonding experience.

Each time I switch on the news, I'm bombarded with more reasons to tuck myself up with a good book and something delicious to eat. Financial meltdown and global warming are both best dealt with from the bedroom. After all, if you're wearing cosy pyjamas and have plenty of blankets you can turn the heating off and, as long as you ban computers from the bedroom, it's impossible to spend any money there.

Some of my earliest memories are my childhood bedroom. When I was very small I had the tiniest bedroom you can imagine. I still remember drifting off to sleep gazing at my teddy bear wallpaper, surrounded by stuffed animals and piles of books. I also remember faking illness, so that I would be given soft-boiled eggs with soldiers which I could eat in the blissful knowledge that all my friends were struggling into starchy school uniform and going out into the cold.

During my teenage years I rarely left my bedroom and spent hours in there reading magazines such as *Blue Jeans* and *Patches* until I graduated to the heady heights of *Vogue* and *Tatler*. It was in my bedroom that I practiced drinking black coffee and cultivating a sophisticated air, while sneaking a very naughty cigarette. I would get up early on a Saturday morning, go downstairs, whip up a plate of scrambled eggs and a cup of Earl Grey and head back to my bed where I'd stay pretty much all day.

My passion for eating in bed has endured and my own children now seem to spend much of their time in their bedrooms. My boys, who used to joke that their eldest sister was a vampire due to her seeming fear of daylight, are now impossible to prise from their own beds at the weekend or during holidays.

If they were allowed to, they'd eat every meal in bed and they often sneak up to their rooms with a pizza or toasted cheese sandwich. Best of all, though, they tell me, are the pancakes I make for them to eat in bed.

When they were smaller, there was nothing they all liked more than piling into our bedroom and eating French toast or muffins and drinking smoothies.

I was thrilled when asked to write this book and decided to try the theory of method writing, so much of this book has been typed in bed and every recipe has been eaten under the covers. Breakfast in bed is blissful, but why stop there? It's lovely to eat in bed at any time of the day, which is why I've added chapters on midnight feasts and duvet days too. After all, if you've got the time why not spend it snuggled up under a duvet?

One shouldn't forget the romantic side of eating in bed. We've been rather brain-washed into thinking that romance requires spending a lot of money, either at smart restaurants or on huge presents. However, I think cooking someone breakfast or rustling up a late-night snack are just as romantic as a statement gift. Joint duvet days, where you both decide to stay home on impulse, can be better than any planned excursion.

A day spent in bed can be as restorative as a trip to the spa and there's no packing required, which frankly has to be a good thing. Having said that, I'm addicted to hotels and feel safer tucked up under hotel linen than anywhere else in the world. As a

cure for disappointment and heartache, few things come close to the sound of a knock on the door and a voice announcing 'room service'. Which is why, at the back of this book, you'll find a list of the best places in the world to eat breakfast in bed [see Romantic escapes, p140].

I've also included a section [see Shopping, p150] where you'll find companies that sell everything from cookware through to nightwear and much else besides. Everything featured in the book can be bought from one of these suppliers.

Getting the food right is, of course, vitally important. It's extremely dull to eat something second rate after you've made the effort to leave your bed for the kitchen and then go back again. No, what you want is something easy to cook, which tastes delicious and looks pleasing. I've included here all the things I, my friends and my family like to eat in bed, which I hope you'll love too.

Setting the scene

When you've got your bedroom absolutely right you'll want to spend more time there than anywhere else. It should offer sanctuary from the outside world, a haven that's peaceful, beautiful, cosy and calming.

A GOOD BEDROOM begins with a good bed. When I first moved out of my parents' home I was told by a very glamorous woman that I should always spend a decent amount of money on my shoes and my bed. "When you're not in one, you're in the other," she said. "And if either is uncomfortable it will show on your face. Show me a woman with wrinkles," she warned, "and I'll show you someone who's scrimped". It's absolutely true – if you're uncomfortable it shows in your face.

If you're planning a bedroom from scratch it's a good idea to begin with the bed. You'll need to decide whether you'd like a divan or a bedstead. A really good divan will probably feel more supportive than a mattress on a bedstead and they often come with drawers underneath, which is brilliant if you're short of storage space. However, a bedstead somehow seems to lend a bedroom much more character and it's possible to pick up some amazing vintage finds.

A bed lasts 10 years on average, so every £100 you spend on your bed represents an investment of around 3p per night. It's worth bearing this in mind when you're standing in the shop looking at what at first appears to be a ruinously expensive option.

Next comes the mattress, which frankly gets more confusing as technology moves on.

Today, as well as sprung mattresses, you can get them made of foam that 'remembers' the shape of your body and moulds to fit you.

It's worth consulting an expert when it comes to choosing both the base and the mattress and if you can get them both from the same place it does make things simpler. Make sure you go shopping dressed comfortably and spend a lot of time trying out the different options. Don't simply hop on and lie on your back. Try out the mattress in all the positions you'd usually sleep in. That way you can see what it'll be like for real.

If you buy a divan bed and you want a smart and finished look, you'll need a headboard. Personally, I don't like bedrooms that look too 'done' so don't favour a headboard upholstered in the same fabric as the curtains. But if you choose a contrasting fabric it can look really great. You'll also, of course, need a valence and for me the same contrasting rules apply.

There are plenty of areas of bedroom design where you can look for cost-saving options, but be warned – if you buy a cheap bed, you'll end up spending more in the long run or suffering sleepless nights for years to come.

Your bedroom should be warm in the winter, cool in the summer, dark enough to

sleep in and laid out practically. As we spend up to a third of our lives in our bedrooms it's important to get every aspect right.

If, every time you enter your bedroom, you are confronted by curtains you feel are a mistake, it'll make your blood pressure rise and will not prove conducive to sleep.

Choosing the colour scheme for your bedroom can be a little tricky. Many people opt for pale neutral or architectural colours on the walls and then liven things up with interesting bed linen. Personally, I like the walls in my bedroom to be really quite dark as I think it makes for a cosier environment.

Bedside tables are a must-have for a comfortable bedroom, but it's imperative not to allow them to become cluttered. I like to have a lamp, a good book, a glass of water and a photograph that makes me happy. I also like to have a scented candle.

There are certain things that have no place in a bedroom and one of them is technology. Having a computer in your bedroom isn't good for either your physical or emotional wellbeing. The same is true of pretty much anything electronic. Many of us have fallen into the habit of using our mobile phones as alarm clocks and leave them right next to the bed. This is a really bad idea – not only are we unsure about their long-term effect on our health, but often they glow with an annoying light that must do something bad to the restful quality of a bedroom.

Bedrooms should offer sanctuary from the outside world, so anything stressful should be kept out. It's rather nice to have a desk in your bedroom – it can double as a dressing table and you can use it to write cards or personal letters. I don't, however, think it's a good idea to use it as the place where you pay bills and deal with the domestic paperwork.

I also think, if there's space, that every bedroom should have a comfortable chair, where you can sit and read a book or simply contemplate life.

The way a bed is made up can make a huge difference to the look of a room and the quality of your sleep. Mattresses should be turned once a month for the first three months when brand new and then every 90 days after that. It should also be regularly vacuumed. It's important to use mattress and pillow protectors; these should be laundered monthly. For extra comfort you can use a mattress topper. There are many different kinds, including memory foam. I think one filled with goose feathers and down is the most luxurious and cosy.

I can't think of anything worse than sheets made from man-made fibres – frankly I'd rather drink ink than sleep on anything nylon, so for me they have to be cotton. Thread count is important, but it's gone a little crazy lately. Anything more than 200 is good and 300 is pretty perfect. You can now buy sheets with a thread count of more than 1,000, but to be honest you'll just spend

lots of money for not much more benefit.

Some people are quite snobbish about fitted sheets, but I find them brilliant. They make making a bed much easier and, if you're the sort who thrashes around at night, then they'll stay put far more effectively.

Even if you use a duvet you should consider using a top sheet – it makes the bed feel much more luxurious. Then comes the tricky one: do you opt for proper blankets or a duvet? The vast majority of us now opt for a duvet, probably because of the comfort factor. I vividly remember getting my first as a teenager. My mother was horrified by the idea of allowing what she called a continental quilt into the house and it took months of persuading before she gave in.

I instantly adored it and until a few years ago, didn't look back. Now, though, I'm feeling nostalgic for the days of blankets with satin edges and am beginning to build up a collection.

When opting for a duvet, it's important to consider the filling. Goose down is considered the smartest and most luxurious as it's warm, light and cosy. A feather and down-filled duvet offers a similar but cheaper option; neither, though, is good for people who suffer from allergies. Silk, however, is and is a great alternative to down. Wool duvets are brilliant for the winter months and are great for anyone who likes a heavier-feeling option. Finally there are duvets filled with synthetic fibres. I don't

like them, but I know many who swear by them, particularly for children's rooms.

It's important not to overlook lighting as it can really spoil a bedroom if you get it wrong. Lighting that's too bright is not conducive either to relaxation or romance and lighting that's too dim will mean you spend hours rummaging for things you cannot see in drawers.

Ideally a bedroom should have a ceiling light and two lamps – one for each side of the bed. The latter should be in easy reach of the bed, as it's truly annoying to have to perform acrobatics each time you want to turn the light off to go to sleep. It's a good idea to use tobacco-coloured lining paper in the lampshades as this creates a flattering golden-coloured light and stops the room from appearing cold. Candles and fairy lights, too, can add a fun boudoir feel.

Then there are pillows. I'm a bit of a pillow diva. Having spent many sleepless nights in hotels or at friends' houses, I now travel with my own pillows, because when they're wrong I find it impossible to sleep. I'm always amused when I hear stories of rock stars' riders demanding over-stocked bars or M&Ms minus the red ones. Should I ever become a world-famous musician (unlikely, but I'm a dab hand on the triangle) I shall demand a day bed, silk-filled pillows and a cashmere blanket.

When it comes to pillows, they are definitely not all created equal. Sleeping on a mean little hard pillow is a hellish experience, which has been known to leave me in tears. In fact, if I were a fairytale character I'd definitely be the princess from *The Princess and the Pea*.

As with duvets, there are a number of different fillings for pillows and some will suit you much better than others. For me, a pillow should be pleasingly plump, but not overly hard, squishy enough to sink into, but not so much that it wraps around the face and tries to smother one.

The best thing is to go to a department store and find an accommodating sales person and get them to take you through the options. Some, I've found, will allow you to take pillows to the bed section and try them out. This, I think, is rather wonderful as I've noticed of late that pillows have suddenly become rather expensive.

Having two large square pillows behind two rectangular ones is rather nice as it gives the bed a very modern look. It's really rather bad for you to have pillows that are past their sell-by date, so here's not an area to scrimp.

Finally, you get to the creative bit of bedroom design and here's where the fun really begins. In an ideal world you should have three sets of linen for your bed. That way you can have one set in the wash, one in the linen cupboard and one on the bed.

This, of course, means that you can change the look of your bedroom each time you change your bed.

As with sheets and pillow cases, duvet covers should be made from cotton or linen and I think are rather nicest when plain white. That way you can use an array of different blankets, throws or pillows to create a unique look.

A bed stacked with pillows is utterly inviting and makes you want to leap on it immediately. Blankets have the same effect. A really beautiful cashmere blanket folded at the end of a bed can look great and is perfect for draping over your shoulders when you're reading in bed. Old-fashioned comforters are great too, particularly if, like me, you like to sleep with your window wide open.

Your bedroom, then, should provide a haven from the outside world and therefore should always be tidy and welcoming. When you step into it, you should feel instantly relaxed and cosseted.

While my kitchen is often in chaos and the drawing room often looks as if there's been some kind of riot in there, I make sure my bedroom is as tidy as it can be – it's where I go to hide from the children, the phone and the dogs.

Once you have created the perfect bedroom, you'll want to spend as much time there as possible and duvet days, midnight feasts and breakfast in bed will all become just that little bit more pleasurable.

PLAIN + PATTERNED PILLOW SLIPS
(OXFORD EDGED)

I regard sleepwear in the way others regard haute couture. My theory is simple: you wouldn't wear the same thing to a wedding as you would to dig the garden, so why would you sleep in the same thing day in day out?

BREAKFAST AT TIFFANY'S is cited as the 'fashion film' and you often see pictures of Audrey Hepburn, as Holly Golightly, on the pages of glossy magazines and style anthologies. Acres of print have been given over to the dresses, sunglasses, hats and accessories that graced the screen, but one never hears mention of the truly fabulous nightshirt she wore. While others have coveted her little black dress, I've always hoped that one day the nightshirt might come up for auction and dreamed that I might even be able to afford to buy it.

Back in the real world, though, I admit that often when I go out to buy a new dress I come back instead with nightwear. Pyjamas have none of the drama associated with them that daywear often has – they need no accessorising, just something to wear over them as you traipse around a chilly house. There's something so cosy, reassuring and stylish about a proper dressing gown, that wearing one somehow makes you feel serene and in control.

We've all been through the phase of wearing a boyfriend's sweatshirt in bed and I think it's rather sweet, but it should end the moment he moves in. Also, anything greying, baggy or where the elastic has gone should be immediately recycled. Most of us have cupboards full of hideous monstrosities that should be replaced with a couple of decent pairs of pyjamas.

Of course, what you wear in bed when you're alone will probably be different to what you wear when you're with someone, but even if it's just you there's no reason for standards to slip. There is, however, nothing worse than a tired robe that has seen better days. I also really rather hate white towelling robes, unless they're worn at a spa or in a hotel room.

White cotton waffle robes are brilliant for the summer, always look smart and are easy to care for. For the winter it's nice to have something much heavier. If you're feeling particularly flush, or have a special birthday coming up, then a cashmere robe is the height of luxury and, properly looked after, should last for years.

I love pyjamas so much I often fantasise about getting home and climbing into mine. There's a fine line, though, between stylishly lounging and looking like a hospital patient, so put as much thought into nightwear as you would into a party dress. Silk pyjamas

are very stylish, but you can't simply throw them into the washing machine, so cotton is much more practical. My favourite of the moment is a rich pink cotton pair with a Mandarin collar and shocking pink piping.

If you're in the first throws of love, it's rather nice to buy one pair of pyjamas between you. He can wear the bottoms and you the top. Many men claim to find a woman sexier in a man's shirt or pyjama top than in a scrap of lace, although most are unlikely to turn their noses up at the latter.

I did a quick poll of my male friends and discovered that a short, slip-style nightdress is the thing most likely to get them hot under the collar, but most said if the option were there, they'd most like a naked woman in their bed. No surprise there then.

Sometimes nothing will do but a pair of flannelette pyjamas. When this urge strikes it's best to give into it. I think it's your subconscious telling you that you need nurturing. If things have gone rather further, you may find that only fleece pyjamas will do the job. If that's the case then make sure you wear them while drinking a mug of hot chocolate – this way you'll ensure you get all the cosseting you need.

Bedwear isn't only for bed –if you've had a long day at work and are feeling frazzled, getting home and climbing into pyjamas as soon as you walk through the door can be relaxing in itself.

Nightwear signifies the end of the day

and the end of your public persona. If, like me, you work from home, you may well find yourself with a freelance wardrobe.

When I worked in an office, I had lots of interesting shirts, tops and jackets. Now I find myself the proud owner of piles of PJs and not much else. There's something rather nice about having a high-powered conference call sitting at the kitchen table in tartan flannelette pyjamas.

It's so much easier for men. It's hard to resist a man in brushed cotton pyjama bottoms and a clean white t-shirt, and a t-shirt and boxers are perfectly acceptable bedwear. I'm also reliably informed by a friend in the know that proper pyjamas from a classic brand are becoming increasingly popular. I think nightshirts on men are seriously cute, but I realise they're not to everyone's taste.

While I don't have a raft of sartorial childhood memories, I do very clearly remember a pair of starchy white cotton pyjamas with Peter Rabbit embroidered on the pocket, which I adored.

I also recall being thrilled whenever I got new sleepwear for Christmas or my birthday. It's something I've tried to continue with my own children and, while I'm happy for them most of the time to live a semi-feral country existence of muddy Converse and ripped jeans, I do prefer it when they go to bed in perfect pyjamas.

When I'm feeling in need of consolation,

I find that pulling on a pair of pyjamas and settling down in front of the fire with a good book is what I really need to get me back on the road to recovery.

Socks are an absolute no-no in bed for men and women, unless they're bed socks, which are a must-have. Cashmere is best and not hideously expensive. Slippers, for both genders, are a tricky area. Choose carefully or you could end up looking like your granny's older sister.

Moccasins are classic and inoffensive and, while I've never met a man who likes marabou mules, I know many women who harbour a secret desire to wear them. Since I had my very first Sindy doll, I've longed for a pair of pink ones like hers.

Sleepwear, then, acts like a punctuation mark in a hectic day and allows you to retreat into your private world. Whatever you decide to wear in bed, as long as you do it with a huge smile and an inner confidence you're sure to look and feel fantastic.

Going undercover
Sleepwear must-haves

Brushed cotton pyjamas of the sort you see in American sitcoms. Brilliant for winter as they're cosy and comforting.

White cotton pyjamas when perfectly crisp and ironed are as smart as bedwear gets.

A white waffle robe is perfect for the summer and conjures up memories of smart hotels.

A heavier robe for winter. Cashmere is the height of luxury and is an investment – properly looked after it will last forever.

Something to seduce in I think I may be allergic to the word negligee, but you know what I mean.

A man's pyjama top is often sexier than a scrap of lace and you'll feel small and feminine when wearing it.

Chanel No 5 After all it's the only thing Marilyn Monroe ever wore in bed!

There's a fine line between stylishly lounging and looking like a hospital patient, so put as much thought into nightwear as you would into choosing a party dress.

BREAKFAST IN BED is undeniably indulgent, whether you do it just for yourself or become a fairy godmother and make breakfast for a houseful. Personally, I love cooking breakfast for a crowd best. I adore the feeling of standing at the Aga, early in the morning, cooking and feeling slightly hungover after a late night of laughing and talking with a bunch of people I love.

I also find it enormous fun to creep from room to room handing out cups of tea to very sleepy friends, before giving them breakfast and cajoling them into a long walk on the beach.

New Year's Day, I think, is one of the best for this kind of gesture. What could be better than starting the year with something yummy prepared by a friend?

Francis Bacon once said "hope is a good breakfast". Actually, perhaps he was misquoted and actually said: "hope it's a good breakfast." Either way, I'm with him.

Breakfast is consoling and comforting. Nothing can seem quite as bleak after a plateful of bacon and eggs.

It's also rather lovely to make breakfast in bed for someone you've rescued from heartbreak or despair.

One morning that lingers in my memory is waking up in my friend Raffaella's house, eight hours after she had tucked me up with

a hot water bottle, and seeing her standing there bearing tea and toast.

Of course, breakfast in bed is just as brilliant, whether you're feeling sunny or sad. For example, I think it's terribly nice to cook something for teenagers after they've had a heavy night out.

You'll seem like the coolest of parents if you gently wake them with food, rather than trying to drag them out of bed at some unearthly hour and forcing them to get their own.

Weekend breakfasts and brunches are something of a ritual in my house. There's a revolt if there isn't something lovely to eat each morning. It's never something I resent. Pottering around in the kitchen while everyone else sleeps makes me feel extremely calm.

The weather, of course, plays a part in what one wants to eat for breakfast. Huge plates piled high with sausages, bacon and eggs with seriously runny yolks are perfect in the depths of winter and leave you feeling properly set up for the day.

In the summer, it's lovely to lounge on top of the duvet eating brioche or gently scrambled eggs, with the windows flung open and the sun streaming in.

For me, the kitchen should be as much a bolt-hole as the bedroom. I firmly believe both should offer an antidote to the stresses of day-to-day life in the 21st century and, approached with the right attitude, cooking can be as relaxing as pretty much anything else. There's an alchemy that occurs in the kitchen when all the ingredients are right and, of course, by that I don't just mean the food.

If you've served a good breakfast then lunch can be much more laid back and simple, as a good breakfast will stave off hunger pangs for a long time.

The key to making breakfast work is for it to be relaxed from start to finish. You need to give yourself time in the kitchen, rather than rushing. I'd rather get up half an hour earlier, drink a mug of tea and put on some really good music and set about cooking in a leisurely fashion.

There's very little pressure on breakfast; while lunches and dinners have all been given the celebrity chef treatment, breakfast still remains firmly in the hands of the home cook, which I think makes it infinitely less stressful as there's nothing to live up to.

Also, while we've all become terribly spoiled when it comes to eating in smart restaurants and are used to friends pulling out all the stops at dinner parties, a great breakfast is somehow rarer and therefore more of a treat. So, what's the point of slaving away to produce something mediocre, when with just a tiny bit more effort you can serve something magical.

Making tracks
Blissful playlist

I always think it's rather nice to have some motivating music playing while cooking breakfast. Here are some ideas.

Buddha of Suburbia
David Bowie

Do You Realize??
The Flaming Lips

Jolene
The White Stripes

Summer (The First Time)
Bobby Goldsboro

It's Different for Girls
Joe Jackson

Jessie
Joshua Kadison

Mary
Scissor Sisters

The Whole of the Moon
Mike Scott and the Waterboys

Pretty in Pink
Psychedelic Furs

Scattered Black and Whites
Elbow

The Full Works

Nothing says 'it's the weekend' like a full English breakfast. I've listed the ingredients per person because it's great to feed your guests a proper breakfast in bed – it'll make them feel as if they're staying in a fabulous hotel.

INGREDIENTS

(Per person)

A little olive oil

2 sausages

2 tomatoes

Sea salt

Freshly ground black pepper

2 rashers of bacon

2 knobs of butter

1 large egg

1 large mushroom

2 slices of toast

Brown sauce
(or ketchup if you must)

METHOD

Pre-heat the grill. Brush the sausages and tomatoes with a little olive oil and season the tomatoes with salt and pepper.

Put the sausages on to grill and allow them to cook for 10 minutes, turning after 5 minutes. Then, carefully slide the tomatoes, cut side up, under the grill tray, so they are beneath the sausages.

Add the bacon to the grill, next to the sausages, and put the pan back under the grill for another 6 minutes or so. You'll need to remember to keep turning the sausages, so the other two sides brown and the bacon should be turned after it's cooked for around 3-4 minutes.

Place a non-stick frying pan with a lid over a medium heat and add a knob of butter and a little olive oil, allowing the butter to melt and start to fizz slightly. Crack the egg into the pan, making sure it has its own space.

Reduce the heat slightly. Cover the pan with the lid and cook for around 4 minutes. The white should cook thoroughly, while the yolk should remain runny on top but be cooked through at the bottom.

While the egg is cooking, fry the mushroom gently in some butter and a little olive oil.

Warm a plate and make the toast. It's best to leave this to the last possible minute, so it remains fresh and warm. Serve immediately.

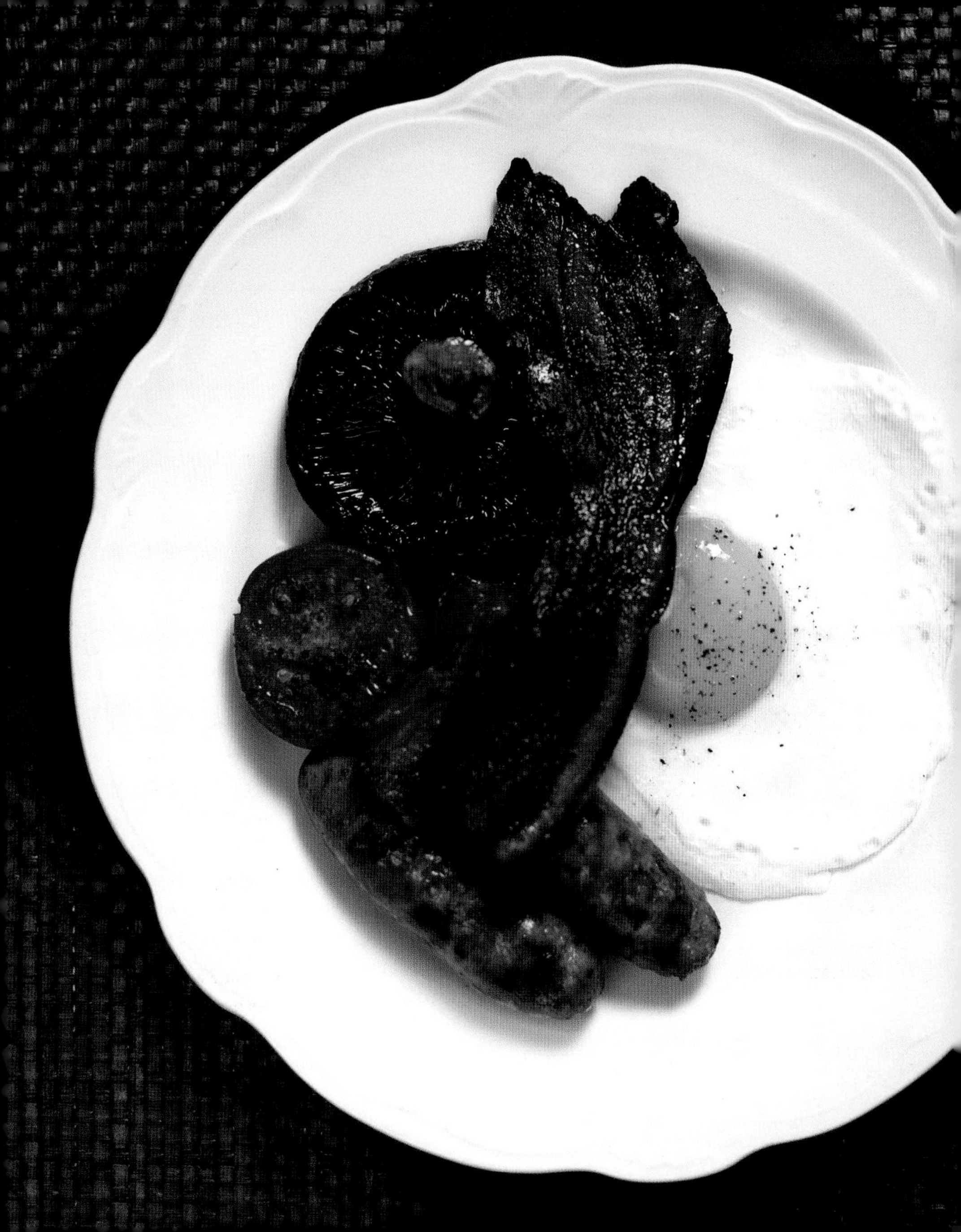

Kippers with Parsley Butter

Kippers are ridiculously easy to cook but utterly divine to eat. I'm convinced that there are few things better for breakfast. Actually, I firmly believe them to be a brilliant hangover cure.

INGREDIENTS

(Serves 2)

2 kippers

4 knobs of butter, chilled

1 tbsp of chopped parsley

1 lemon, cut into half

METHOD

Pre-heat the grill to just over halfway. Put one knob of butter on to each kipper and grill them for about 4 minutes or until lightly coloured.

Turn the kippers over and grill for another 4-or-so minutes.

Serve the kippers on warm plates and place one of the remaining knobs of butter on each.

Sprinkle the parsley on top of the butter and serve with a lemon half.

Kedgeree

There's something a little decadent about a breakfast of kedgeree. I like to make it when we have lots of people staying. Often we'll eat it around the kitchen table, but I also rather love the feeling I get when I deliver it to guests in bed.

INGREDIENTS

(Serves 4)

3 large eggs

450g undyed smoked haddock

150ml full-fat milk

25g butter

1 tsp olive oil

1 onion, finely chopped

$^{1}/_{4}$ tsp ground coriander

$^{1}/_{4}$ tsp ground cumin

$^{1}/_{4}$ tsp turmeric

175g basmati rice

Handful of chopped, fresh coriander

2 limes, cut into wedges

METHOD

Kedgeree is one of those dishes that has a number of elements, so it's best to multitask and get all the elements cooking at the same time. It's best to start by boiling the eggs for around 10 minutes.

Place the haddock in a shallow pan and cover it with the milk, then cook on a medium heat for about 6 minutes, until it's cooked through.

Take the fish out of the pan, keeping aside the milk. Flake the haddock, getting rid of any skin and bones and cover it with foil so it stays warm.

Melt the butter in a saucepan that has a lid and add the oil to stop the butter from burning. Add the onion and spices and cook until the onion softens.

Add the rice and stir well. Once the rice is coated, add a ladleful of the milk you'd set aside and top up with 400ml of salted water.

Bring to the boil and then put the lid on the pan and simmer for about 10 minutes until the rice is cooked through.

Quarter the hard-boiled eggs and add them, along with the flaked haddock, to the pan.

Sprinkle over the coriander and carefully stir the kedgeree, taking care not to squash the eggs.

Serve with lime wedges.

Cinnamon Toast
with Berry Compote

Unless you're feeding a huge crowd there'll be plenty of compote left over, but you can pop what remains in the fridge and eat it for pudding with ice cream or use it to spice up plain yoghurt.

INGREDIENTS

(Per person)

For the cinnamon toast

2 slices thick white bread

Butter

$1/2$ tsp ground cinnamon

1 tbsp of golden caster sugar

For the compote

Large knob of butter

3 tbsp unrefined caster sugar

2 tsp vanilla extract

Punnet of strawberries

Punnet of raspberries

Punnet of blueberries

METHOD

Pre-heat the grill.

Toast the bread on one side, under the grill. Butter the untoasted side.

Mix the cinnamon with the sugar and sprinkle it on the buttered side of the toast.

Put the toast back under the grill and cook it for 30-60 seconds or until the sugar has melted and started to bubble. A word of warning here: be careful not to burn your fingers, it's unbelievably painful to have melting sugar stuck to your finger.

For the compote, melt the butter over a low heat. Stir in the sugar and vanilla extract.

Cook gently until the sugar has melted.

Pop in the fruit and shake the pan. Cook for around 4-5 minutes or until the fruit starts to soften.

Pancakes with Bacon and Maple Syrup

There's something quintessentially spoiling about eating pancakes in bed.

INGREDIENTS

(Serves 2)

115g plain flour

Pinch of salt

Pinch of sugar

1 tsp baking powder

3 eggs, lightly beaten

140ml full-fat milk

Knob of butter

4 rashers of streaky bacon

Maple syrup for drizzling

METHOD

Sift the flour into a bowl and add the salt, sugar and baking powder. Make a well in the middle and gradually add the eggs and then the milk, mixing as you go.

Alternatively – and this is my preferred option – you can blitz all the above ingredients together in either a blender or mixer.

Leave the mixture to stand, while you melt a little of the butter in a frying pan and cook the bacon. Keep the bacon warm once it's cooked.

Grease a small frying pan with some of the remaining butter and pour in some of the pancake mixture.

Once the pancake starts to rise and bubble, turn it over and cook for a minute or two on the other side.

Remove the pancake and keep it warm. Repeat until you have used up all the mixture.

Pile the pancakes onto two plates and criss-cross the bacon over the top.

Drizzle with maple syrup and serve immediately.

Brioche

So elegant, so French, so yummy and everyone will be hugely impressed that you made it yourself. Delicious served warm and dripping with butter or homemade jam.

INGREDIENTS

(Makes 6)

150g white bread flour, plus extra for dusting

Pinch of salt

30g caster sugar

1 x 7g sachet of easy-blend dried yeast

2 medium free-range eggs, beaten

40ml warm milk

75g butter, softened, plus extra for greasing

METHOD

Sift the flour and salt into a bowl, then stir in the sugar and yeast. Make a well in the middle and add most of the eggs. Pour in the milk.

Mix the ingredients together with your hands to make a dough, slowly adding the butter until you've used it all.

Put the dough on a floured board and knead for 5 minutes until you have a springy ball (the dough should be shiny). Alternatively, throw the above ingredients into a mixer and beat with a dough hook for about 5 minutes.

Place the dough in a large bowl and cover the bowl with clingfilm. Chill in the fridge for at least an hour or overnight if making well in advance.

If you have individual brioche tins, you'll want to use these. If not, you can use a muffin tray. Whichever you choose, you'll need to grease it.

Divide the dough into equal portions, kneading as you go and forming them into rounds. Place the brioches into the tins and leave in a warm place until they've doubled in size. About 15 minutes before you plan to begin baking, pre-heat the oven to 200ºC/gas mark 6 .

Brush the brioches with a little of the leftover beaten egg. Pop them in the oven and bake for 12-15 minutes or until golden brown and risen.

Remove from the oven and allow to cool on a wire rack before eating.

Strawberry and White Chocolate Muffins

These are probably my most favourite muffins ever.

INGREDIENTS

(Makes 6)

1oz butter

3 tbsp vanilla syrup

1 egg

4 tbsp full-fat milk

Punnet (about 400g) of strawberries, hulled and quartered

150g good white chocolate, smashed into small pieces

150g plain flour

1 tsp baking powder

$^1/_2$ tsp bicarbonate of soda

You will need

6 muffin cases

METHOD

Pre-heat the oven to 180°C/gas mark 4.

Melt the butter in a bowl over a saucepan of water on the hob.

Once it's melted, mix it with the vanilla syrup and egg and add the milk.

Mix the dry ingredients together in a bowl, then add the butter, syrup and egg mixture.

Add the chocolate and strawberries and gently mix together.

Line a muffin tin with the cases and spoon in the mixture.

Bake in the oven for 25 minutes.

Delicious served warm or cold.

Blueberry Scones

Blueberries say breakfast to me more than any other fruit. And since they're meant to cure everything from disease to wrinkles, you can feel smug while you're eating.

INGREDIENTS

(Makes 6)

225g self-raising flour

Pinch of salt

55g butter

25g caster sugar

175g blueberries

150ml full-fat milk, plus a little extra for brushing

METHOD

Pre-heat the oven to 220°C/gas mark 8.

Lightly grease a baking sheet.

Mix together the flour and salt and rub in the butter.

Stir in the sugar and the blueberries. Add the milk and stir further to get a soft dough.

Turn onto a floured work surface and knead very lightly. Pat the dough into a square, about 4cm thick.

Using a floured knife, cut the dough into squares and then into triangles.

Brush the top of each triangle with a little milk.

Bake for 15-20 minutes until well risen and golden.

Allow to cool on a rack.

Serve with really good butter.

Eggs Benedict

I defy anyone not to love this classic breakfast dish. While making the Hollandaise sauce can seem a little daunting, if you use the processor method below it's actually plain sailing and little can go wrong.

INGREDIENTS

(Serves 2)

4 egg yolks

Salt and freshly ground black pepper

1 tbsp lemon juice

3 tbsp white wine vinegar

200g butter

Splash of hot water

2 whole eggs

4 slices streaky bacon

2 muffins

METHOD

To make the Hollandaise sauce you first need to put the egg yolks into a blender or food processor and add a good pinch of salt and pepper. Add a splash of water and whizz for at least a minute.

Heat the lemon juice and the vinegar in a small saucepan until it starts to bubble then turn the blender on again and add the lemon and vinegar mixture to the eggs, very slowly, and whizzing all the time.

Melt the butter in a saucepan until it begins to foam and then slowly add it to the sauce in the processor, a little at a time.

Continue to blend until the sauce thickens, adding the hot water if it becomes too thick. Keep it set aside.

Fill a shallow pan with about 4cm of water and bring it to a simmer, then add a splash of vinegar.

Break each egg into a glass, then gently tip them into the water. Allow them to poach in the simmering water for about three minutes. Remove and drain on some kitchen towel.

Grill the bacon until it's crispy, then lightly toast the muffins.

Place an egg on each muffin, 2 slices of bacon on the egg and then pour over the Hollandaise sauce.

Fried Herring's Roe

There's a café close to me that serves this dish and I have become a complete addict. I love it best when the bread goes a little soggy. We're lucky to live near two brilliant fishmongers, so I make sure it's often on the menu at home.

INGREDIENTS

(Serves 2)

150g plain white flour

Sea salt

Freshly ground black pepper

250g herring's roe, de-veined

Splash of olive oil

150g butter

4 slices thick white bread

METHOD

Pour the flour on to a plate and season it with salt and pepper.

Toss the herring's roe in the flour and then spread them out on another plate.

Pour a little olive oil into a frying pan add the butter and allow it to melt over a medium heat.

Once the butter is sizzling, add the herring's roe and cook, turning occasionally until they're firm and golden brown all over.

Toast the bread and butter it.

Put the herring's roe on top of the toast and eat it while it's hot.

Homemade Muesli

This is a world away from the slightly 'cardboardy' shop-bought version and takes less than 20 minutes to make. It stores well in an airtight jar, so if you'd like to make more you can just multiply the quantities given here.

INGREDIENTS

(Serves 4)

200g jumbo porridge oats

25g wheat germ

75g rye flakes

50g hazelnuts, crushed

50g flaked almonds

50g raisins

50g dried apple, chopped into small chunks

50g dried figs, chopped into small chunks

METHOD

Pre-heat the oven to 160°C/gas mark 2.

Put the oats, wheat germ, rye flakes and nuts on a baking tray and toast for 5 minutes.

Turn over the ingredients and toast for a further 5 minutes.

Remove the tray from the oven and leave its contents to cool.

Once it's totally cool, mix in the fruit.

Eat the muesli with ice-cold milk and a sprinkling of brown sugar.

Flapjacks

Great as a breakfast snack. I often serve flapjacks with a pot of tea to get house guests through to brunch. They're also marvellous for breakfast on the move.

INGREDIENTS

(Makes 8 slices)

15g butter, plus extra for greasing

50g unrefined caster sugar

4 tbsp golden syrup

250g rolled oats

METHOD

Pre-heat the oven to 190°C/gas mark 5.

Grease and line a shallow square tin with baking paper or Bake-O-Glide.

Put the butter, sugar and golden syrup in a small pan over a low heat and cook until the butter has melted, stirring all the time.

Stir in the oats. Press the mixture into the tin and bake for 20 minutes or until the flapjack mixture is just golden around the edges.

Remove from the oven and allow to cool completely before turning out the flapjack and cutting into squares with a sharp knife.

Ayurvedic Porridge

This is my breakfast of choice when I'm feeling virtuous or in need of something pure and cleansing. It's surprisingly delicious and extremely good for you.

INGREDIENTS

(Serves 1)

275ml milk

110g rolled oats

Pinch of ground cinnamon

2 cubes of crystallised ginger, finely chopped

METHOD

Pour the milk into a non-stick saucepan and bring it to the boil.

Stir in the oats and cinnamon.

Bring to a very gentle simmer and cook for around 5 minutes, stirring occasionally.

Once the mixture is cooked, stir in the crystallised ginger and serve immediately.

Romantic breakfasts

When it comes to sharing food, I've always thought breakfast in bed so much more romantic that a candlelit dinner in a smart restaurant. There's an intimacy that's bound up in the nurturing act of having prepared the food yourself that's unique and special.

YOU REALLY KNOW someone loves you when they traipse down the stairs on a chilly morning, cook you something lovely and bring it back to bed for you. In these straightened times, it's the small gestures that'll keep us together.

The great thing about breakfast is that it needn't be complicated, you don't have to be a brilliant cook and you don't need tons of ingredients. Plus, some things can be prepared in advance, so you needn't spend hours in the kitchen.

Small touches make a big difference, a hand-written note on a tray, a flower picked from the garden, or pebbles collected from the beach often mean more than a grand gesture. I remember reading somewhere that love is an action not a feeling and if the act is to cook something delicious and nurturing, then I'm all for it.

There are few things as enchanting as the first few months of a new love affair, when every waking moment is spent thinking about the object of your affections and your dreams are haunted by them.

Sadly, once you get to the stage where you're sharing a gas bill, you can find that your romantic get-up-and-go has got up and gone. If you've got to that stage in your relationship, then routine and ritual can take the place of high drama and, in

the long run, be far more romantic.

Weekend breakfast is the perfect time to begin. If you make a date to spend every Sunday morning in bed, you'll find it really bonding. You can take turns to cook breakfast and I promise, it'll become something you really look forward to.

I realise the sheer impossibility of this if you have very small children and your Sunday mornings begin early when they climb into your bed and wriggle and giggle until getting up seems a more peaceful option. However, if at all possible ship them off to their godparents, grandparents, family or friends at least a couple of times a year and take to your bed.

I'm an incurable romantic, in love with being in love. I adore the fact that music sounds better, strawberries taste sweeter and the sun shines brighter simply because you're spending time with someone who makes you swoon.

So cooking breakfast for someone I'm besotted with and getting cosy really suits my nature. But, I'm very aware that the food I cook doesn't need to be ridiculously elaborate, even a boiled egg and soldiers is always hugely appreciated. However, if you want to push the boat out, choose goose eggs instead of chicken and asparagus instead of bread for the soldiers.

I'm an incurable romantic, in love with being in love. I adore the fact that music sounds better, strawberries taste sweeter and the sun shines brighter simply because you're spending time with someone who makes you swoon.

Love is a funny old thing. Often it's the things we adored about someone in the beginning that drive us crazy later. I believe that if you can just keep talking, you can get over most things. But because we live our lives at a hectic pace, time for this kind of communication is often short. Which is why taking the time to eat breakfast in bed together can be all it takes to keep your relationship on track.

According to Robert Graves, one of the symptoms of love is leanness and I totally relate to that. I know many people who find it impossible to eat when they're falling in love – or indeed going through tough times.

So if you're beginning a relationship with someone whose appetite disappears somewhere during the run-up to the first kiss and doesn't resurface for some months, the kindest thing you can do is to make sure you feed them delicious morsels on a regular basis. Small pancakes or mouthfuls

of omelette are somehow easier to cope with mid-swoon than a huge plateful of food that requires rather a lot of attention.

Small acts of kindness are the glue that holds a relationship together. Waking your beloved with a cup of tea, will guarantee they think nice things about you all day.

Men seem to fall into two camps when it comes to romance. There are the ones that are always there, roses in hand, grand gesture at the ready and lines smoothly delivered with perfect timing. And then there are the kind who declare themselves unqualified to practice romance, but make you feel safe and cosy nevertheless.

From what I've seen the former are more likely to run off with your best friend and the latter to be there in the long run. But perhaps the best way to tell if you have managed to bag a good one is to see if he brings you breakfast in bed.

One thing that the new austerity seems to have done is to have made us appreciate

the small things much more and to value authenticity in our relationships and realise the importance of real love.

Every love affair needs its own soundtrack and I firmly believe a romantic breakfast is hugely enhanced by the right songs playing in the background. I love it when you hear a song on the radio that immediately transports you back to a moment in time.

If that moment happens to be a lazy Sunday morning spent sprawled across the bed drinking Bellinis then, frankly, it doesn't get much better than that.

It's perhaps for this reason that I'm rather addicted to creating playlists that are perfect for every occasion. I find it hugely relaxing and enormous fun.

I realise that may make me sound like the 21st century version of someone who arranges their CDs in alphabetical order, but it's so nice to be driving somewhere and to choose a playlist that will make you feel all the wonderful things associated with being in love.

If you're the sort of couple who spend every minute of the weekend water skiing or sky diving, you may find the idea of a romantic breakfast in bed a little tame, but it can be hugely thrilling and blissfully lovely.

I can't think of anyone who wouldn't be hugely touched by the one they love going to the effort of surprising them with a delicious breakfast.

Making tracks
Romantic playlist

Every love affair needs a soundtrack and where better to listen to it than in bed while eating something delicious.

Riverman
Nick Drake

Girl
The Beatles

Perfect Day
Lou Reed

Ain't No Sunshine
Bill Withers

Dream
Dinah Washington

Drive
The Cars

Everything
(is never quite enough)
Wasis Diop

Without You
Harry Nilsson

We're all the Way
Eric Clapton

A Kiss to Build a Dream On
Louis Armstrong

53

Soft-boiled Duck Eggs
with Asparagus

Everyone can boil an egg and cooking asparagus is terribly easy, so if you're looking to do something romantic why not try this?

INGREDIENTS

(Serves 2)

2 duck eggs

8 asparagus spears

METHOD

Fill a saucepan with water and bring to the boil. Put in the duck eggs and boil gently for around 12 minutes.

Trim the woody ends off the asparagus. Bring a large pan of water to the boil. It should be big enough to allow you to lay the asparagus down in it.

Place the asparagus in the pan and bring back to the boil. Lower the heat to a gentle simmer and cook until the asparagus bends a little, but not so long that it becomes floppy. It should take about 7 minutes.

Lift the asparagus out of the water and drain on some kitchen towel.

Serve immediately and eat, propped up on pillows, using the asparagus as soldiers.

Scrambled Eggs with Smoked Salmon

The thing about scrambled eggs – apart from the fact that they taste delicious – is that they're very easy to make and, when you add a slice of smoked salmon, they suddenly feel rather luxurious.

INGREDIENTS

(Serves 2)

3 large eggs

30ml double cream

Salt and freshly ground black pepper

15g butter

2 large slices of smoked salmon

2 slices of bread for toasting

METHOD

Crack the eggs into a bowl, add the cream, salt and pepper and whisk gently with a fork.

Melt the butter in a small, heavy-based pan over a medium heat.

When the butter begins to bubble, pour in the eggs. Let them sit there for about 30 seconds, then begin to gently stir with a wooden spoon.

Keep stirring off and on until they're almost cooked, but still runny in places.

Remove the pan from the hob and allow the eggs to continue to cook in the pan away from the heat.

After a minute or so, serve the scrambled eggs on hot buttered toast, with the slices of smoked salmon artfully arranged on top.

Buckwheat Pancakes with Caviar

This is a truly extravagant breakfast, but all love affairs should drift into lavish territory at least once. You can, of course, trade the caviar for smoked salmon and it will still be delicious.

INGREDIENTS

(Serves 2)

300ml full-fat milk

7g sachet of easy-blend yeast

1 tsp sugar

25g buckwheat flour

175g strong plain flour

1 tsp salt

2 eggs, separated

25g butter

100ml crème fraîche

50g caviar

METHOD

Gently warm the milk in a pan on the hob and stir in the yeast and sugar. Leave to stand for 10 minutes.

Sift the flours and salt into a mixing bowl and make a well in the middle.

Slowly beat in the milk mixture and egg yolks. Cover and leave in a warm place for at least an hour.

Whisk the egg whites until they become stiff and fold them into the batter.

Add a little butter to a large frying pan and heat on the hob.

Spoon a little batter into the pan to make a small circle and repeat until the batter is all used, ensuring you leave space between each pancake.

Cook for around 30 seconds on each side.

Place a little caviar on each pancake and serve with crème fraîche on the side.

Spinach & Mushroom Omelette

I think this is a pretty perfect breakfast for lovers to share as you're eating two halves of the same thing. It will also ensure you have lots of strength for any mid-morning romping you may choose to engage in.

INGREDIENTS

(Serves 2)

Olive oil

Butter, for frying

Handful of mushrooms, chopped

Handful of spinach leaves

4 eggs

1 tbsp double cream

Salt and freshly ground black pepper

4 tbsp grated Cheddar

METHOD

Heat a little olive oil and butter in a frying pan and fry the mushrooms, stirring frequently until they start to become golden.

Add the spinach and sauté it gently until it wilts. Drain any excess liquid and set aside the mushrooms and spinach.

Heat some more butter in a heavy pan on a gentle heat on the hob. Put the eggs into a bowl and gently worry them a bit. This is different from frantic beating or enthusiastic whisking – it's much gentler and will stop the omelette tasting rubbery.

Add the cream and season with salt and pepper.

When the butter starts to foam, pour the egg mixture into the pan. As the egg begins to set, gently prise the corners away from the side of the pan and sprinkle over the cheese, ensuring it covers the whole omelette.

Then put the mushrooms and spinach on one side of the omelette. Allow the omelette to cook for another few minutes until it's just about set – it should be slightly golden underneath and the cheese should be melted.

Angle the pan and fold the omelette in half. Tip the omelette onto a plate and cut it in half.

Serve with buttered bread.

Omelette Arnold Bennett

It's said the brilliant Arnold Bennett wrote an entire novel while staying at the Savoy and, while he toiled, the hotel's chefs created his perfect omelette. It, in turn, makes the perfect romantic breakfast.

INGREDIENTS

(Serves 2)

175g smoked haddock

1 litre full-fat milk (for poaching the haddock)

2 tbsp butter

2 tsp flour

150ml full-fat milk

125g freshly grated Parmesan

Salt and freshly ground black pepper

1 egg yolk

1 egg white

4 whole eggs

METHOD

Put the haddock in a saucepan and pour over litre of the milk. Simmer over a gentle heat for about 6-8 minutes or until the fish is cooked.

Flake the fish from the bone and set it aside.

Melt 1 tbsp of the butter in a small saucepan over a low heat. Remove the pan from the heat and stir in the flour to make a roux. Return the pan to a low heat and stir in a little milk.

Once it's blended in smoothly, add a little more milk and stir again, then repeat until just over half the milk has been used.

Stir in the rest of the milk and $^3/_4$ of the Parmesan.

Continue to stir until the mixture thickens, then season with a little salt and some pepper and stir in the egg yolk. Leave to cool.

Pre-heat the grill to high. Beat the egg white in a large bowl until it forms stiff peaks and set aside. In another bowl, gently beat the whole eggs.

Heat the remaining butter in a frying pan, over a medium heat. When it begins to bubble, stir in the haddock and pour over the whole, beaten eggs.

Tip the pan around to ensure good egg coverage then cook for a couple of minutes.

As the egg begins to set, prise the corners from the side of the pan, tilting the pan to let any liquid egg into the gaps. Stir the beaten egg white into the Parmesan sauce.

Remove the pan from the heat and spread the sauce mixture on top of the omelette, then put the pan under the grill for about 40 seconds.

Take it out and sprinkle the remaining Parmesan over the top of the omelette and grill for another minute or two or until the surface begins to brown.

Slide the omelette from the pan on to a warmed serving plate and cut into slices.

I like this best served with thickly buttered brown bread and a green salad.

Poached Eggs with Smoked Haddock and Spinach

Smoked haddock and poached eggs are one of those culinary marriages that just works – the creaminess of the yolk and the saltiness of the fish combine to create breakfast heaven.

INGREDIENTS

(Serves 2)

2 small smoked haddock fillets

1 pint full-fat milk

Splash of white wine vinegar

2 eggs

1 bag spinach

METHOD

Put the haddock in a saucepan and pour over the milk.

Simmer over a gentle heat for about 6-8 minutes or until the fish is cooked.

Meanwhile, fill a shallow pan with about 4cm of water and bring it to the simmering point, then add a splash of vinegar.

Break each egg into a glass, then gently tip them into the water and allow them to poach in the simmering water for about three minutes.

Remove them with a slotted spoon, then drain them on some kitchen towel.

Heat a frying pan on the hob on a medium heat, then add the spinach and allow it to gently wilt.

Warm two plates and layer with the spinach, the smoked haddock and a poached egg on top.

Serve immediately.

Angels on Horseback

You're meant to either love or hate oysters and I've done both, going from being horrified at the idea of them to eating so many one night it caused people to talk. There is, however, no denying the romantic associations.

INGREDIENTS

(Serves 2)

8 fresh oysters, shucked
(but keep the shells)

Salt and freshly ground
black pepper

4 rashers of streaky bacon

Bread for toasting

You will need

8 cocktail sticks

METHOD

Pre-heat a medium grill.

Season the oysters with a little
salt and pepper.

Cut each bacon rasher in half
and wrap a piece around each
oyster.

Secure with a cocktail stick.

Cook under the grill for
5 minutes, turning once.

Then return each oyster to the
shell and serve with warm
toast.

Pancake Hearts
with Strawberries

This is thoroughly kitsch and should be served wearing a frilly apron and with a huge helping of irony. After all, if you can't be silly when you're in love, when can you be?

INGREDIENTS

(Serves 2)

75g plain flour

Pinch of salt

Pinch of sugar

$^1/_2$ tsp baking powder

2 eggs, lightly beaten

80ml full-fat milk

Knob of butter

Handful of strawberries, hulled and cut in half

METHOD

Sift the flour into a bowl and add the salt, sugar and baking powder.

Make a well in the middle and gradually add the eggs and then the milk, mixing as you go.

Alternatively – and this is my preferred option – blitz all of the above ingredients together in either a blender or mixer.

Grease a small frying pan with some of the butter and put it on the hob over a medium heat.

Make the pancakes as you normally would by pouring the batter into the frying pan.

Once the pancake starts to rise and bubble, flip and cook for a minute or two on the other side. Remove the pancake and keep it warm.

Repeat – greasing the pan with butter each time – until you have used all the mixture and have a pile of warm pancakes.

Then, using a heart-shaped cookie cutter, cut out lots of little heart shapes and arrange them on the plate with the strawberries.

Sprinkle over some sugar and serve to the love of your life with a huge smile.

Ideas for Bellinis

There are few things as romantic as the sound of a champagne cork popping and, as it's so easy to make a Bellini, you're guaranteed to impress even if you serve one of these with a boiled egg. Each makes enough for two.

Classic

INGREDIENTS

1 peach, peeled and
de-stoned

Chilled champagne

METHOD

Put the peach in a blender and blitz until you're left with a smooth purée.

Put the peach purée in the bottom of the champagne flutes and top up with champagne.

Serve at once.

Lychee

INGREDIENTS

40ml lychee purée

40ml lychee liqueur

Chilled champagne

METHOD

Mix the lychee purée and lychee liqueur together and pour into a champagne glass.

Top up with chilled champagne and serve at once.

Strawberry

INGREDIENTS

10 strawberries

2 tbsp sugar

Chilled champagne

METHOD

Put the strawberries in a pan with the sugar and some water.

Cook on a gentle heat until the strawberries become really mushy. Pass the mixture through a sieve and chill it in the fridge for around 30 minutes. Pour some strawberry purée into champagne flutes, until they're about $1/3$ full. Top up with chilled champagne and stir. Serve at once.

Perfect Bloody Mary

The perfect accompaniment to a romantic breakfast. If the night before was heavy, then a large one will perk you up. If you were tucked up early and had a full eight hours of sleep, you deserve something with a bit of a kick.

INGREDIENTS

(Serves 4)

300ml vodka

Dash of sherry

Dash of Worcestershire sauce

Dash of Tabasco

700ml tomato juice

Pinch of celery salt

Juice of 1 lime

METHOD

Simply pour all the ingredients into a jug and stir.

Waffles with Caramelised Bananas

These are very easy and cooked bananas are among the most delicious tastes.

INGREDIENTS

(Serves 2 hungry people)

75g plain flour

Pinch of salt

Pinch of sugar

$^1/_2$ tsp baking powder

2 eggs, lightly beaten

80ml full-fat milk

Knob of butter

4 bananas, peeled and cut in half lengthways

2 tbsp icing sugar

Maple syrup, to serve

You will need

A waffle iron

METHOD

Pre-heat a grill to high for the bananas.

Sift the flour into a bowl and add the salt, sugar and baking powder.

Make a well in the middle and gradually add the eggs and then the milk, mixing as you go.

Alternatively – and this is my preferred option – blitz all of the above ingredients together in either a blender or mixer.

Allow the batter to rest while you heat the waffle iron. Grease with a little of the butter.

Add a ladelful of batter and cook until done. Keep the first waffles warm, while you make the others.

Dust the bananas with some of the icing sugar and place them under the grill until they're golden and caramelised.

Put two banana halves on each waffle, dust with further icing sugar and drizzle over some maple syrup.

Family breakfasts

One of the things I've loved most about having children is the opportunity to indulge and cosset them. With life lived at a crazy pace, weekend breakfasts provide just that opportunity. It's the small things they'll remember when they grow up, such as the ritual of making pancakes every Saturday morning.

I DON'T NECESSARILY go in for twee food designed especially for children. Nor, however, do I believe children's eating habits are entirely down to their parents. Two of my children will eat anything and are very adventurous. Another, though, balks at the idea of anything more adventurous than a baked potato with cheese and is extremely fussy, finding the idea of trying anything new very daunting indeed.

To me it seems odd. All of my children have had the same experience with food, yet their attitudes couldn't be more at odds with each other. The recipes I've included in this section should not prove tricky for those children who are nervous about food, but should equally be loved by those who are food adventurers.

They're also recipes the children can help with, should they feel so inclined. The arty ones, such as Turtle Pancakes (see page 84), have thrilled my own children as well as those who've been visiting. They find the challenge of getting it just right interesting and often decide that the turtle currently in the pan, would benefit from a nifty little hat, or perhaps the next one should not be a tur- tle at all, but a rabbit instead.

I also know many people turn up their noses at the idea of allowing children to eat anything as sugary as doughnuts for breakfast. While I agree that this would be bad if it happened every day, I do think it's utterly desirable on an occasional basis, as a special treat.

Actually, I'd go further and say that I worry for the emotional health of children not allowed to eat anything containing sugar and who reach the age of 10 not knowing what chocolate tastes like. To me it seems not only mean, but dangerous; how will a child learn moderation if never given the chance to practice it?

When it comes to everyday breakfasts, my children – like most others – eat mainly toast, cereals and the odd boiled egg. But, if a weekend passes and they haven't eaten pancakes, they tend to look rather neglected and can complain very loudly indeed.

Muffins are another thing children are usually very fond of – partly, I believe, because they're easy to make and don't require a huge amount of precision or mixing. I also find most children are intrigued to find ingredients as prosaic as flour and milk can turn into something quite so fun and delicious.

It shouldn't be forgotten that children are by nature generous little people who adore indulging in grown-up activity. Both of these traits can be brought to the fore if they're allowed to cook breakfast in bed for a tired

or stressed-out mother or father.

I remember my youngest son sneaking downstairs at 5am on his father's birthday and waking us up with a plate of underdone, unbuttered toast. The look of pride on his face when he handed us the plate made it such a treat. He talked for days about the fact that he'd managed to surprise his dad.

If you'd like something just as charming, but infinitely more edible, then it's a good idea for the other parent to be in on the surprise – and the cooking. But of course they should allow the child to take all the credit. Now my children are so much older, I miss the Sunday mornings when they leapt into our bed demanding food and cuddles. Now I'm lucky to see them before 11:30am and breakfasts have become brunch. But then my eldest daughter, who is at university, still strives to come home most weekends, as much for the food as for the company.

I adore it when friends come to stay and bring their small children as it's such fun to allow the parents some much needed sleep by encouraging their children into the kitchen and allowing them to make French toast or some other treat for their parents.

Childhood is fleeting and it's the small things that you and they remember about the early years. Perhaps it says something about my gluttony, but for me many of the small things I remember are based around thrilling the children with delicious food.

Making tracks
Family playlist

I believe it's as important for children to be introduced to a wide variety of music as it is for them to be fed good food. This feels like a pretty good start.

Witchita Lineman
Glen Campbell

The Outdoor Type
The Lemonheads

I've Been to a Marvellous Party
The Divine Comedy

Golden Touch
Razorlight

Nothing Rhymed
Gilbert O'Sullivan

Livin' Thing
The Beautiful South

Sloop John B.
The Beach Boys

No Ordinary Girl
Counting Crows

White Rabbit
Jefferson Airplane

Wake up Boo!
The Boo Radleys

French Toast

This is the first recipe my daughter Lucie ever attempted alone, which makes me hugely nostalgic. Every time I eat it, I remember her as an adorable six-year-old rather than the stunning teenager she has grown into.

INGREDIENTS

(Serves 2)

2 large eggs

60ml full-fat milk

$1/2$ tsp vanilla extract

$1/4$ tsp ground cinnamon

4 thick slices of white bread

Butter, for frying

Honey, for drizzling

METHOD

Beat together the egg and the milk. Add the vanilla extract and cinnamon and mix well.

Soak the bread in the egg mixture for a minute or so, ensuring both sides are covered.

Heat the butter in a frying pan over a gentle heat and fry the bread for a couple of minutes, before turning it over and frying the other side.

Repeat until you've used all the bread.

Drizzle each slice of bread with honey and serve.

Breakfast Bap

I have no idea why, but I always feel there's something slightly sleazy about this (in a good way). Maybe it's because it's the thing I crave when I've stayed out all night and have arrived home still in my dress and heels.

INGREDIENTS

(Per person)

1 sausage

Sea salt

Freshly ground black pepper

Half a tomato

1 rasher of bacon

Knob of butter

A little olive oil

1 large egg

I floury roll

Brown sauce
(or ketchup if you must)

METHOD

Pre-heat the grill to the high side of medium.

Put the sausage on to grill and allow it to cook for 6 minutes, turning every couple of minutes.

Season and carefully slide the tomato, cut side up, under the grill tray, so it is beneath the sausage.

Add the bacon to the grill, next to the sausage and put the pan back under the grill for another 6 minutes or so.

You'll need to remember to keep turning the sausage, so the other two sides brown and the bacon should be turned after it's cooked for around 3-4 minutes.

Place a non-stick frying pan with a lid over a medium heat and add the butter and a little olive oil, allowing the butter to melt and start to fizz slightly.

Crack the egg into the pan, making sure it has its own space. Reduce the heat slightly. Cover the pan with the lid and cook for around 4 minutes. The white should cook thoroughly, but the yolk should remain runny on top and be cooked through at the bottom.

Butter the roll. How you assemble your breakfast bap is entirely personal, but I cut the sausage in half and put it at the bottom, place the tomato on top, then the bacon, then the egg, then a dash of brown sauce and then put the lid on!

79

Pigs in Blankets

This is a recipe one of my American friends makes when she comes to stay. In England, we tend to think of pigs in blankets as sausages wrapped in bacon. They have them in Germany, too, and they're called sausages in nightgowns.

INGREDIENTS

(Serves 6)

1 packet of puff pastry

6 hot dog sausages

I egg, beaten with a little milk

METHOD

Pre-heat the oven to 200°C/gas mark 6.

Roll out the pastry until it is about 5mm thick and cut it into triangles big enough to cover most of the sausage, but just leaving the ends exposed.

Wrap a piece of pastry around each sausage. Brush with the egg wash and put onto a baking tray lined with baking parchment.

Cook in the oven for 10-15 minutes until they're golden brown.

Serve immediately.

Turtle Pancakes,
page 84

Turtle Pancakes

It's important to encourage small children to get involved in the kitchen and, as anyone with little ones knows, they like nothing more than being creative. You can make any animal and if you can't do it free-hand you can use cookie cutters.

INGREDIENTS

(Serves 4)

115g plain flour

Pinch of salt

Pinch of sugar

1 tsp baking powder

3 eggs, lightly beaten

140ml full-fat milk

Knob of butter

TIP If you're using cookie cutters, put them in the pan with the butter and carefully pour in the batter. Once it begins to bubble, remove the cookie cutter carefully and turn over the pancake to cook the other side. Once you've cooked the first batch, keep them warm and start again.

METHOD

Sift the flour into a bowl and add the salt, sugar and baking powder. Make a well in the middle and gradually add the eggs and then the milk, mixing as you go. Or – and this is my preferred option – blitz all the above ingredients together in either a blender or mixer.

Grease a small frying pan with some of the butter and put it on the hob over a medium heat.

If you're making turtle shapes, then first spoon in some batter creating a medium-sized oval shape which will form the body. It's easier than it sounds. You need to use a ladle and pour a longish shape and the batter will naturally move outwards thus creating the oval

shape you're looking for. Next, add a head to the top of the body and then four flippers and, of course, a small tail.

All of this sounds rather unwieldy, but you'll find it takes less than a minute.

Once the pancake starts to rise and bubble (particularly on the tail, which you added last) turn it over and cook for a minute or two on the other side.

Remove the pancake and keep it warm. Repeat – greasing the pan with butter each time – until you have used all the mixture. If you make a mistake, you can always tidy it up with a knife at the end.

Serve with maple syrup, lemon and sugar or strawberries.

Banana Muffins

While most children love the flavour of bananas, many of them dislike the texture, so these muffins are a great way to make sure they benefit from their natural goodness.

INGREDIENTS

(Makes 8)

200g plain flour

$^{1}/_{2}$ tsp baking powder

$^{1}/_{2}$ tsp bicarbonate of soda

Large pinch of salt

3 ripe bananas

150g unrefined caster sugar

1 egg

50ml full-fat milk

75g unsalted butter, melted

$^{1}/_{2}$ tsp vanilla extract

METHOD

Pre-heat the oven to 180°C/gas mark 4.

Put the flour, baking powder, bicarbonate of soda and salt in a bowl and mix it together .

In a separate bowl, mash the bananas and mix in the sugar, egg, milk, butter and vanilla extract.

Fold in the dry ingredients and mix until everything is combined (don't worry about lumps, as a slightly lumpy mixture makes better muffins).

Spoon the mixture into muffin cases in a muffin tin.

Bake the muffins in the oven for 25-30 minutes or until they are golden in colour and spring back when lightly pressed.

Serve warm with some natural yoghurt.

Plum Muffins

I am hideously spoilt, living within walking distance of Back to the Garden – the best farm shop in Norfolk. Perhaps the best perk is that pretty much every day I eat something cooked by the talented Keith Wyatt, who created these fab muffins.

INGREDIENTS

(Makes 10)

750g red plums, de-stoned

75g unrefined caster sugar

3 tsp ground cinnamon

480g plain flour

1 tsp baking powder

$1/2$ tsp bicarbonate of soda

Pinch of salt

200g caster sugar

2 eggs

280ml natural yoghurt

110g butter, melted

Icing sugar

METHOD

Pre-heat the oven to 180°C/gas mark 4.

Put the plums in an ovenproof dish, sprinkle over the unrefined caster sugar and 2 tsp of the ground cinnamon and swirl everything around a bit.

Bake for 15 or so minutes until the plums are soft and the skin splits. If they're not at this stage, put them back for another 5 minutes.

Remove them from the oven, put them on a plate and allow them to cool.

Put all the dry ingredients, minus the caster sugar, but including the remaining tsp of ground cinnamon, into a bowl and combine. Put the sugar, eggs, yoghurt and butter into a another bowl and whisk them together.

Add the plums and then casually mix the wet and dry ingredients together. You can be fairly relaxed with this because with muffins you don't need everything to be carefully blended.

Put some muffin cases into a muffin tray and spoon in the mixture. Bake for 25-30 minutes.

Dust with icing sugar before serving.

Chocolate Bread

I know chocolate for breakfast is very naughty, but this tastes so great and it's enormous fun to get the children into the kitchen to help make it. It's particularly yummy still warm from the oven.

INGREDIENTS

(Makes 1 loaf)

650g strong white bread flour

1 tsp salt

$^1/_2$ tsp sugar

7g sachet of instant-dried yeast

5 tbsp cocoa powder

Good splash of olive oil

200ml full-fat milk

200ml warm water

175g good chocolate, smashed into small bits

METHOD

Mix together the flour, salt, sugar, yeast and cocoa powder.

Make a well in the centre of the dry ingredients. Pour in the olive oil, water and milk and combine until a dough is formed.

Turn out on to a lightly floured surface and knead for about 10 minutes.

Put the dough back into the bowl and cover it with a clean tea towel. It needs to go somewhere warm to rise – an airing cupboard is perfect.

Leave the dough for about an hour or until it has doubled in size.

Take it out of the bowl and pound it until it deflates.

Mix the smashed chocolate in well, trying to ensure even coverage.

Shape the dough into a loaf shape and place it in a 1kg loaf tin or on a baking tray.

Put the dough back in the warm place and leave for another 30 minutes to rise.

Put the tin or tray in an oven that has been pre-heated to 220°C/gas mark 8 and bake for about 35 minutes or until the bread looks baked and sounds hollow when tapped on the base.

Nutty Banana Hot Chocolate

One of my children discovered this while away on a school trip and it's become a breakfast staple. Oddly, even as they're getting older, none has yet grown out of it and, if I'm honest, I rather love it myself.

INGREDIENTS

(Serves 2)

2 bananas

2 tbsp peanut butter

Five large squares of milk chocolate

Four tbsp double cream

600ml full-fat milk

METHOD

Put the bananas and peanut butter into a blender

Melt four squares of chocolate in a saucepan over a low heat. It's really important to do this gently.

With the saucepan still on the heat, mix in the cream, beating quickly with a spoon.

Add the banana and peanut butter purée. Then add the milk slowly, a little at a time, still beating, until you've used it all.

Turn up the heat a fraction and warm the hot chocolate until it's very hot, but not boiling.

Pour the hot chocolate into two mugs and grate over the top the remaining square of chocolate.

Banana Smoothie

This tastes heavenly and is a good way to get children to eat bananas if they're fussy about the texture.

INGREDIENTS

(Serves 2, but just multiply the ingredients for more)

2 bananas

1 pint full-fat milk

4 ice cubes

1 tbsp honey

$^1/_2$ tsp vanilla extract

METHOD

Put all the ingredients in a blender, whizz until smooth and pour into glasses.

My children love it if I put a cocktail umbrella in the glass.

Doughnuts

Warm doughnuts covered in sugar remind me of walking on Brighton Pier as the sun goes down over the water, which is why they've become a breakfast staple – I can almost smell the salty air when I take a bite.

INGREDIENTS

(Makes around 24)

75ml milk

75ml water

50g butter

250g strong white bread flour

$\frac{1}{2}$ 7g packet instant-dried yeast

150g caster sugar

1 egg, beaten

METHOD

Warm the milk and water with the butter in a saucepan until the butter has almost melted.

In a separate bowl, mix together the flour, salt, yeast and 30g of the sugar (putting the rest aside for later).

Add the egg to the butter and milk mixture and stir, then pour it all into the dry ingredients and combine, first with a wooden spoon, then with your hands.

Knead the dough for 10-15 minutes (this is actually blissfully relaxing).

Put the dough into a lightly greased bowl, cover with a tea towel and put it somewhere warm – an airing cupboard is ideal– until it has doubled in size. This will definitely take more than an hour, maybe even two.

Punch the dough and knead it again, ensuring it becomes smooth and silky.

Divide the dough into small pieces and roll into rounds in your hand.

Pre-heat the deep fat fryer to 180ºC and, once the oil is ready, pop in the doughnuts a batch at a time. They'll probably take around 8 minutes to cook and you'll need to flip them once to ensure they brown all over.

When they're out of the fryer and still warm, roll them in the sugar. Eat them as soon as you can, as they're most delicious when warm.

Lucy's Great Granola

I cannot claim credit for this recipe as it belongs to my friend, the brilliant Lucy O'Donnell. She's so talented that she eventually set up the company Lovedean, which makes granola commercially.

INGREDIENTS

(Serves 2)

250g jumbo oats

100g honey

35g pecan pieces

35g hazelnuts

35g brazil nuts

30g sunflower seeds

30g pumpkin seeds

30g hemp seed

30g linseed

20ml sunflower oil

15ml pumpkin oil

METHOD

Pre-heat the oven to 220°C/gas mark 8.

Mix all the ingredients together and spread them across two baking sheets.

It's really important that you take the baking sheets out of the oven every few minutes or so and turn the ingredients over to ensure everything gets evenly golden.

Lucy's golden rule is: 'no burning, keep turning'.

It'll take around 20 minutes to cook.

Lucy's granola tastes amazing when served straight from the oven with semi-skimmed or soya milk on a cold winter's morning.

Alternatively, you can serve it cold with yoghurt, chilled semi-skimmed or soya milk.

It's also delicious sprinkled on porridge.

Duvet days

Duvet days are my favourite days. After all,
what's the point of weekends and holidays if
you don't spend at least some of them in bed?
Taking time out is both restful and restorative
and, frankly, important for your
emotional wellbeing.

I FIRMLY BELIEVE that the odd duvet day is vital for keeping your sanity intact. Disappointment, rejection, heartbreak and malaise are best dealt with under the covers. When you're feeling so low that you can't quite face the world, then don't. Batten down the hatches and take to your bed.

There's a right way and a wrong way of doing it, though. Staying in bed wearing a grubby t-shirt, with unwashed hair and refusing to eat anything other than junk food is not the way forward. Self-loathing is bound to creep in and you'll find yourself thinking it was no wonder you were dumped, your boss rejected your presentation and even the dog doesn't like you.

A well-spent duvet day includes the following: crisp, clean bed linen; great pyjamas; a well-stocked fridge; a pile of good books; and an iPod stacked with songs that you can sob along to as well as those guaranteed to help you get your mojo back.

How and what you eat is important if you're feeling awful. Munching only on chocolate will play havoc with your blood sugar levels and will ultimately leave you feeling worse than you did in the first place. You need good, wholesome food that will help you keep your strength up.

It's when you're in need of a duvet day

that you'll either thank your lucky stars that you've done your bedroom up perfectly, or mourn the fact that you haven't. As I've said before, it's good to have three sets of bed linen for your bed – one on, one in the wash and the other in the linen cupboard. If you're having a duvet day then a good way to begin is by changing your bed, then hop in the bath with some lovely bubbles. After that, change into clean pyjamas, go into the kitchen, fix some breakfast and climb back into bed with a good book.

I used to believe that miserable duvet days were best spent flicking through *Vogue*, but I've since changed my mind. While there is no better magazine for a happy duvet day (yes they do exist), when I'm feeling sad it feels all a bit much to subject myself to pictures of beautiful people wearing clothes I most definitely cannot afford. Instead, I've realised that books are the way forward.

Of course, a double duvet day is infinitely more fun than one spent alone. So if you can persuade the love of your life to take the day off and spend it tucked up under an eiderdown, then this is definitely a good move. It's a bonding experience and, if you are both cutting out of important meetings, it'll make you feel slightly naughty and as if you were teenagers again.

It's important, though, to agree

beforehand what you want to get out of the day. If he's cutting work because he wants to watch football or re-runs of *Top Gear* all day and you had visions of romantically feeding each other strawberries dipped in chocolate and gazing dreamily into each other's eyes, one of you will be disappointed.

A duvet day should mean time out, so it's a good idea to ban mobile phones from the bedroom. You should only take a laptop if you intend to use it to watch a film.

On that subject, *Breakfast at Tiffany's* is the perfect duvet day film whenever you take to your bed. If you're suffering in love *Sliding Doors* is a good bet and has the best haircut scene in cinema history. If you're looking for something to make you sob, films don't come much better than *The Lives of Others*. And, if you want to get cosy and connected then watching *Brief Encounter* or *An Affair to Remember* should do the trick.

If you're alone and suffering, smother your face and body in lotions and potions, paint your nails and make sure that even if you're heart is shattered into tiny pieces you're looking your best. After all, if he has a change of heart and comes hammering on your door, he'll see what he's missing.

If you're together, then luxuriate in the time away from ringing telephones, e-mail and all of the other pressures that life throws at you. Pretend you're the last people on earth and remember why you got together in the first place.

Making tracks
Duvet day playlist

There's little point in having a duvet day unless you're going to stack your iPod with songs to comfort and console.

The Stranger Song
Leonard Cohen

How's it Gonna End?
Tom Waits

Blue Moon
Billie Holiday

Going to a Town
Rufus Wainwright

Some Riot
Elbow

One for my Baby
Frank Sinatra

Sara
Bob Dylan

Letter to Hermione
David Bowie

Last Goodbye
Jeff Buckley

Hurt
Johnny Cash

Duvet Day books for her…

Mallory Towers – Enid Blyton
Any of the books from the Mallory Towers series will leave you inspired to become as plucky as Darrell Rivers and are guaranteed to leave you feeling soothed, ready for anything.

Charlotte Sometimes – Penelope Farmer
One of the stars of the time-slip genre, it makes you believe anything is possible and nothing is quite what it seems.

The Falling – Elizabeth Jane Howard
The insidious menace of the male lead will probably lead to your forgiving the man who has wronged you as you decide that compared with Henry, he's rather nice after all.

Summertime – Raffaella Barker
If you live in town this book will make you want to move to the country and if you live in the country it will simply leave you feeling a little smug. The sumptuous descriptions of weather and landscape mean you needn't leave your bed to experience the elements.

Breakfast at Tiffany's – Truman Capote
The book is much darker than the film and probably even more enjoyable. Holly Golightly is the original blonde bombshell and not the sort to take a broken heart lying down. Definitely the one to read if you've lost your romantic mojo.

…and for him

A Confederacy of Dunces – John Kennedy Toole
This is a book that must appear on the have-read list of every man, so why not devour it in one sitting while under the duvet.

Young Stalin – Simon Sebag Montefiore
This rich and gripping, award-winning biography is the perfect book to get lost in.

King Solomon's Mines – H. Rider Haggard
This is a real man's book and a perfectly brilliant pick-me-up.

High Fidelity – Nick Hornby
I don't think I know a man who couldn't relate to Rob. Any man who loves music – particularly recorded on vinyl – or women should take to his bed immediately and read this.

Touching the Void – Joe Simpson
Whatever has driven you to your bed will pale into insignificance when compared to the traumas laid out in this gripping and terrifying true story. You'll also be thrilled to find yourself safe in bed!

The Hidden Man – Charles Cumming
This compelling tale of espionage is a thinking man's thriller that will keep you gripped from the very first page.

Cheat's Herb Risotto

A good risotto is the most consoling dish in the world. I also believe it's rubbish that you have to stand over it ladling in hot stock. If you'd rather be soaking in a hot bath while the risotto takes care of itself, this is how to do it.

INGREDIENTS

(Serves 2)

1 tbsp olive oil

$^1/_2$ a large white onion, chopped

200g Arborio rice

$^1/_2$ a glass of white wine

500ml chicken stock

Salt and freshly ground black pepper

25g butter

Handful of torn basil leaves

Handful of chopped chives

150g Parmigiano cheese, grated

METHOD

Preheat the oven to 140°C/gas mark 1.

Heat the olive oil in a heavy-bottomed saucepan that has a lid. Add the onion and cook it until it's soft. This should take about 10 minutes.

Add the rice and stir so it becomes coated in the oil and onion.

Add the wine (this makes a very satisfying sizzling sound) and continue to cook until the wine has almost all evaporated.

Add the stock and a little salt and pepper and bring to the boil. Remove the saucepan from the heat and put the lid on.

Put it in the oven for around 15 minutes until the stock has almost been absorbed and the rice is *al dente*.

Stir in the butter, herbs, and cheese.

Go back to bed and enjoy!

Leek and Potato Soup

I have absolutely no idea why it should be, but I find the act of making and eating soup seriously therapeutic. Maybe it's because soup is easy to make and easy to eat and there's a rhythmic nature to both.

INGREDIENTS

(Serves 4)

1 tbsp olive oil

$^1/_2$ a large red onion, chopped

100g potatoes, peeled and chopped

1 large leek, sliced

600ml chicken or vegetable stock (I prefer chicken)

Salt and freshly ground black pepper

75ml double cream

METHOD

Heat the olive oil in a large pan on a medium heat on the hob and add the onion, potatoes and leek.

Cook for 3-5 minutes until they begin to soften, but do not brown.

Add the stock and bring to the boil.

Season with salt and pepper and simmer until the vegetables become tender.

Pour the soup into a blender and whizz until smooth.

Pour into a clean saucepan, stir in the cream and heat through.

Smoked Haddock Soup

If you're feeling too miserable to leave your bed or can't face the cold outside, then this soup is perfect – it's rich, comforting and offers real solace. Serve with rustic bread and lashings of really good butter.

INGREDIENTS

(Makes enough for two, or one all day)

5 Maris Piper potatoes, peeled

2 tbsp olive oil, not extra virgin

3 large leeks, sliced

1 large red onion, finely chopped

320g smoked haddock

500ml fish stock

150ml double cream

Freshly ground black pepper

20g chives, chopped

METHOD

Put the potatoes in a pan of boiling, salted water and cook until they're tender. Drain them and cut them into smallish chunks.

Heat the olive oil in a saucepan and cook the leeks and onion over a medium heat, until they're soft.

Add the stock and bring it to a gentle boil. Add the potatoes and haddock and simmer for about 8 minutes until the fish begins to flake.

Stir in the cream and season with pepper.

Scatter over the chives and serve.

Chicken Soup

It's a well-known fact that chicken soup can cure anything and everything. From hangover to heartbreak, a couple of spoonfuls of this golden liquid will set you on the road to recovery.

INGREDIENTS

(Serves 4)

8 chicken pieces

2 sticks celery, chopped

8 carrots, peeled and cut in half lengthways

2 parsnips, peeled and roughly chopped

1 swede, peeled and cut into large chunks

1 large white onion, peeled and cut into large chunks

1 bouquet garni

4 litres of water

6 tbsp Osem chicken-flavoured soup powder

Salt and freshly ground black pepper

METHOD

Put all the ingredients into a large stock pot and bring to the boil.

Reduce the heat and skim off any impurities, which appear on the surface as a scum.

Stir well, then allow the soup to simmer for at least 2 hours (longer if you have time), skimming every now and then.

Carefully remove the chicken pieces and pass the soup through a fine strainer.

You can now serve the soup or allow it to cool and then put it in the fridge for later.

You can serve with dumplings, chopped carrots and noodles for authenticity.

Season to taste.

Arancini

Arancini – which means little orange – is traditionally eaten mid-morning in Italy. This recipe was given to me by my friend, Keith, who cooks up delicious treats for the farm shop next door. They're scrummy hot or cold.

INGREDIENTS

(Makes 4-6 balls)

1 large white onion, finely diced

50g butter

320g Arborio rice

100ml dry white wine

1 litre of vegetable stock

Handful of Cheddar, grated

Sweet chilli sauce

1 ball of Mozzarella

Plain flour, for dusting

2 eggs, beaten

Breadcrumbs

METHOD

Soften the onion in the butter, then add the rice and stir.

Add the wine and simmer, stirring continuously, until all the alcohol has been cooked off.

Add the vegetable stock a ladleful at a time. Stir all the time, only adding further stock when the previous amount has been fully absorbed by the rice.

Simmer for about 20 minutes, until the rice is creamy and fluffy, but still has some bite. At this point, remove from the heat.

Stir in the Cheddar and leave to cool.

Once the rice has cooled, put aside about $^1/_5$ of the rice, then shape the rest into balls about the size of a small orange.

Make a hole in each ball and add into each space $^1/_2$ tsp of sweet chilli sauce, followed by a chunk of Mozzarella. Seal the hole in each of the Arancini balls with the rice set aside earlier.

Dust each Arancini ball in flour, then roll in the beaten eggs and coat with breadcrumbs.

If you have a deep-fat fryer, deep-fry at 170°C/gas mark 3.5 for 8 minutes until beautifully golden.

Alternatively, you can shallow-fry them, turning occasionally, until they're golden.

Fried Gefilte Fish

The thing I love most about Jewish food is its ability to comfort and console.
Fishballs – as they're colloquially known – are so delicious that I often find
myself mindlessly eating them until I've polished off an entire plateful!

INGREDIENTS

(Makes around 20)

$^1/_2$ a large white onion,
roughly chopped

1 carrot, peeled and roughly
chopped

2 eggs

2 tsp salt

2 tbsp caster sugar

500g white fish fillets

50g matzo meal

Vegetable oil for frying

METHOD

Put the onion, carrot, one of
the eggs, salt, sugar and the
fish in a food processor and
whizz until the mixture
becomes mushy and well
blended.

Then pop it in the fridge for
about half an hour.

Wet your hands and begin
forming the mixture into small
balls. You'll need to keep
wiping and wetting your hands.

Break the remaining egg into a
bowl and beat it well.

Pour the matzo meal on to a
large plate. Dip each fish ball in
the egg and then roll in the
matzo meal until it's covered
all over.

Pour enough oil into a pan that
it will cover the fishballs and
heat it until it's very hot.

Fry the fishballs in batches
until they're golden brown.

Allow them to cool (if you can)
before diving in.

Thai Noodles

This is real boy food, so all my girlfriends talk the men in their lives into taking a duvet day by promising to cook this and watch *Top Gear* on a loop, which seems jolly kind indeed.

INGREDIENTS

(Serves 2 hungry people)

120g rice stick noodles

2 tbsp olive oil

2 eggs, beaten

1 red chilli, finely chopped

2 garlic cloves, finely chopped

Juice of 1 lime

2 tbsp fish sauce

1 tsp sugar

150g large prawns, chopped

200g chicken, sliced into strips

2 spring onions, finely chopped

150g bean sprouts

50g peanuts, crushed

METHOD

Soak the noodles in warm water for 10 minutes.

Heat 1 tbsp of the olive oil in a wok and pour in the beaten eggs.

Swirl them around a little and allow them to cook rather as if they're becoming an omelette.

Remove from the wok and cut into small pieces.

Add the chilli and garlic and cook for half a minute, before adding the fish sauce, lime juice and sugar, then cook for another 30 seconds.

Add the prawns and chicken and cook for around 4 minutes or until they're almost cooked through. Add the spring onions and bean sprouts and cook for another minute or two.

Drain the noodles and tip them into the wok.

Give everything a good stir and allow the noodles to heat through.

Serve in bowls and sprinkle over the crushed peanuts.

Sausage, Bacon & Potato Hash

This is seriously soothing when you feel strung out, stressed or a bit wobbly.

INGREDIENTS

(Serves 2)

3 medium potatoes, chopped into 1.5cm chunks

1 Spanish onion, peeled and sliced

4 pork and leek sausages, sliced

1 tbsp olive oil

4 rashers of streaky bacon, chopped

Salt and freshly ground black pepper

METHOD

Bring a pan of salted water to the boil and cook the potato chunks for until they're tender – this should take 7-9 minutes.

Drain them and set them aside.

Heat the oil in a pan add the sausage slices and cook for a few minutes on each side until they're cooked through and are nicely coloured.

Remove them from the pan and add the onions and gently fry them until they soften, but don't burn.

Add the bacon and fry for a few seconds before adding the potatoes.

Fry the potatoes until they become golden and the bacon crispy.

Pop the sausages back into the pan and cook for another few minutes until they're piping hot.

Season to taste and tuck in!

Gingerbread Ice Cream

Brilliant for emergencies of the emotional kind. Ever since my teenage years I've been feeding it to girls with man trouble and it never fails to work. I'd save it for serious heartbreak as you'll want to experience the full benefit.

INGREDIENTS

(Serves 2)

75g unsalted butter

50g dark muscovado sugar

2 tbsp golden syrup

150g plain flour

$\frac{1}{2}$ tsp bicarbonate of soda

2 tsp ground ginger

1 large tub of vanilla ice cream

METHOD

Pre-heat the oven to 170°C/gas mark 3.5.

Line a baking tray with baking parchment. Melt the butter, sugar and syrup in a medium saucepan, stirring occasionally. Remove the pan from the heat.

Sift the flour into a bowl and add the bicarbonate of soda and ginger.

Stir the wet ingredients into the dry ones and make a dough.

Lightly flour a work surface and roll out the dough. Cut into squares and then place them on the baking tray.

Bake the gingerbread for 9-10 minutes until it turns a lovely golden brown.

Leave the gingerbread to cool and take the ice cream out of the freezer to soften.

When the gingerbread has cooled sufficiently, smash it into bits (this is very satisfying if you've been cruelly treated), then put the ice cream into bowls and mix in the gingerbread.

Vanilla Custard

Consoling, creamy, reminiscent of childhood and the most divine shade of yellow, what is there not to love about custard? Even the word is beautiful. Eat this when you're feeling low and it's sure to perk you up.

INGREDIENTS

(Serves 2)

125ml single cream

125ml full-fat milk

1 vanilla pod

3 egg yolks

20g caster sugar

Bananas, chopped into slices, to serve

METHOD

Put the cream and milk into a small saucepan. Split the vanilla pod and scrape the seeds into the saucepan with the milk and cream and then add the pod. Heat until almost, but not quite, boiling.

Meanwhile, mix the egg yolks and sugar together in a heat-proof bowl.

Take the saucepan off the heat and slowly whisk the milk and cream mixture into the egg mixture, a little at a time, until it is all used up.

Take a heavy-bottomed pan and pour in the custard, stirring continuously for about 10 minutes.

When the custard has thickened, pass it through a sieve into a bowl.

Serve with chopped-up bananas.

Chocolate Cake

When you're eating chocolate cake all feels right in the world. The whole point of a duvet day is to make you feel safe, warm and cosy, so it makes a lot of sense to indulge in a large slice of chocolate cake at some point during the day.

INGREDIENTS

(Serves 4)

250g softened butter

250g unrefined caster sugar

4 eggs

1 tsp vanilla extract

3 tbsp good quality unsweetened cocoa powder

250g self-raising flour

4 tbsp full-fat milk

30g good quality milk chocolate

30g good quality dark chocolate

30g good quality white chocolate

METHOD

Pre-heat the oven to 180°C/gas mark 4.

Beat together the butter and sugar until you get a light and creamy mixture.

Break the eggs into a bowl, add the vanilla extract and mix.

Gradually beat the eggs into the butter and sugar mixture. Sift the cocoa powder and flour into the mixture, add the milk and, using a metal spoon, gently fold in until it's fully blended.

Smash the chocolate into small pieces and add to the cake mixture.

Pour the mixture into a greased 20 x 4cm round cake tin.

Bake for 30-40 minutes or until the cake springs back when gently pressed in the centre and has shrunk away from the sides of the tin.

Turn the cake out on to a wire rack and let it cool.

Banana Bread

As my children grow up, I mourn the passing of their childhoods, consumed by the memory of their pudgy arms plunged into mixing bowls as we spent another wet Sunday afternoon in the kitchen. This was always a favourite.

INGREDIENTS

(Makes 1 loaf)

60g butter, cubed

120g caster sugar

Large pinch of salt

360g self-raising flour

1 large egg

125ml full-fat milk

4 ripe bananas, chopped into 2cm rounds

METHOD

Preheat the oven to 180°C/gas mark 4.

Grease a 1kg loaf tin with a little of the butter (make sure you leave 50g aside).

Put the sugar, salt and the self-raising flour in a mixing bowl. Make a well and add the egg, milk and remaining butter and mix together well.

Alternatively, throw all of the above ingredients into a mixer.

Add the bananas to the mixture and, using a spoon, fold them in. Put all the mixture into the loaf tin, making sure you catch every last drop from the bowl.

Put the tin on the middle shelf of the oven and bake for 50 minutes, before testing with a skewer. If it comes out clean and the loaf has risen and is a lovely golden colour, then it's done.

If the skewer comes out with any of the mixture on it, then you should put it back for 10 minutes before testing again.

Remove the tin from the oven and allow the loaf to cool for about 5 minutes before turning it out onto a cooling rack.

Best eaten warm, with lashings of butter.

Midnight feasts

Midnight feasts should always be exciting.
Whether you're eight or eighty, they should
make you feel young, irresponsible and
decadent. The best kind, I think, are at the
beginning of a relationship when you feel
dizzy with the heady romance of it all.

MIDNIGHT FEASTS – even the words conjure up a decadent atmosphere. As a child there's something so thrilling about being able to stay up late and greedily tuck into something yummy. It's a thrill that hasn't diminished now that I'm grown up.

I don't know why but I've always found the time between midnight and falling asleep really potent. It's as if there's a possibility that anything might happen. I know some people adore leaping out of bed early in the morning and watching the sun rise, but I feel much more alive in the deep dark night.

There are many different types of midnight feasts and everyone should experience each kind at least once.

There are the lust-fuelled kind, where you've enticed someone seriously gorgeous into your bedroom only to find you're both too ravenous to ravish each other until you've had something sustaining to eat. Actually, as this usually happens before you know each other terribly well, you can use it as an opportunity to seriously impress by making sure you effortlessly whip up a signature dish, rather than attempting something complicated for the first time.

Then there are the type you share with a group of friends after a big night out or when you're staying in a cottage in the wilds, where the only entertainment is conversation,

board games and whatever you can find in the fridge. I love this kind of night, particularly if the wind is howling outside and someone is lyrically telling a ghost story.

As well as remembering the firewood, it's actually a good idea to plan a midnight feast as there's something deliciously childish in getting excited making the arrangements.

There are midnight feasts that you share with your children, when they're small enough to be enthralled by being allowed to eat by candlelight. My children always beg me to tell them stories of my childhood adventures when we do this and I find it a really sweet and bonding experience.

And there are the kind you eat with your best friend, when one of you has been disappointed in love. These are usually Bridget Jones-style affairs and often involve a large tub of ice cream. It's a good idea to ensure you also cook something nutritious and full of protein as a sugar rush and heartbreak are a bad combination.

Finally, there are the committed couples kind, where you lie in bed both feeling hungry until one of you makes it to the kitchen to whizz up some scrambled eggs for you to both eat under the duvet. While it is, of course, brilliant to plan a midnight feast, the spontaneous ones are often the best. You know the sort when you think there's

nothing in the kitchen to eat, but you manage to throw something together from leftovers in the fridge and it tastes wonderful.

I can't decide which my favourite is because they're all rather wonderful. Perhaps it simply depends where in your life you are at that particular moment.

Just as making breakfast in bed can be a hugely romantic gesture, so can rustling up a midnight feast. I firmly believe that food is the way to anyone's heart and therefore feel the need to feed everyone at every available opportunity, even in the middle of the night.

The key to getting a midnight feast right is to know what you're aiming for. If it's simply to cure late-night hunger, then there are lots of quick and easy things you can do. If you're going all out to impress you need to think about it more carefully, but the food doesn't need to be too tricky.

It's also about the atmosphere you create and the care you put into it will inform how it all works out. In some ways the lighting, music and mood are as important as the food. If you're trying to help a friend recover from a broken love affair you need to keep everything muted and cosseting; if seduction is your aim you need to ramp up the volume a little and pull out all the stops.

I guess the most important thing about a midnight feast is for everyone to embrace the spirit of doing something that's a little bit naughty to ensure that the whole thing is enormous fun.

Making tracks
Midnight playlist

Midnight feasts should be infused with romance and the songs you play should add to the sleepy, late-night feel.

Mr Tambourine Man
Bob Dylan

Steppin' Out
Joe Jackson

Iris
The Goo Goo Dolls

I Wonder Who's Kissing Her Now
Ray Charles

One More Cup of Coffee
Robert Plant

Cyprus Avenue
Van Morrison

My Funny Valentine
Chet Baker

Win
David Bowie

A Rush of Blood to the Head
Coldplay

On an Island
David Gilmour

123

Welsh Rarebit

Although you're risking strange dreams by eating cheese late at night, I really can't think of anything I prefer more as a midnight feast. This is quick, easy and tastes exceptionally good.

INGREDIENTS

(Makes 2 slices)

150g Caerphilly

4 tbsp Guinness

1 tsp English mustard

$^1/_2$ tsp Worcestershire sauce

1 tsp flour

2 slices crusty white bread

METHOD

Gently heat the Caerphilly, Guinness, mustard and Worcestershire sauce in a saucepan on the hob.

Allow the cheese to melt and all the ingredients to meld together.

Once this has happened, stir in the flour and mix until you have a paste. Allow it to cool totally.

Toast the bread and then spread the paste over one side of each slice.

Place the toast under a pre-heated grill and cook until the topping browns.

Mushrooms on Toast

Mushrooms on toast takes me back to when I was a teenager. My best friend at the time was a girl called Helena and we would come back from parties and cook this, while trying not to wake anyone up.

INGREDIENTS

(Serves 2)

2 tbsp olive oil

Knob of butter, plus a little for spreading

2 cloves of garlic, finely chopped

4 large mushrooms, sliced

120ml double cream

1 tbsp flat-leaf parsley, finely chopped

2 slices of lovely bread

METHOD

Heat the olive oil and butter in a frying pan over a medium heat and add the garlic.

Cook for a minute or two, then add the mushrooms and cook for another 5-7 minutes, stirring occasionally.

Add the cream to the pan and bring to a simmer and sprinkle over the parsley.

Meanwhile, toast and butter the bread.

Serve the mushrooms on the toast.

Scallops in Garlic and Parsley Butter,
page 128

Scallops in Garlic and Parsley Butter

Easy to prepare, quick to cook and utterly delicious.

INGREDIENTS

(Serves 2)

8 scallops

Sea salt and freshly ground black pepper

100g butter

2 fat cloves of garlic, finely chopped

1 teaspoon finely chopped flat-leaf parsley

METHOD

Scallops are ridiculously easy to cook, but it is important you do it correctly. If they're quite thick, it's a good idea to cut them in half as then you can be sure they'll cook evenly but won't be overcooked.

Season the scallops with salt and pepper.

Melt the butter in a large frying pan until it starts to bubble. Add the garlic and cook for about 2 minutes.

Add the scallops to the pan, making sure each has lots of space. Sprinkle over the parsley and cook the scallops for 2-3 minutes.

Turn over the scallops and cook them on the other side for another 2 or so minutes.

Place the scallops on plates and pour over the garlicky butter sauce.

Serve with thickly cut chunks of wholemeal bread and a green salad.

Spaghetti Carbonara

I first wrote down this recipe about 10 years ago when I had the odd job of writing about food and seduction for a dating magazine. I suggested it as something to try if you were simultaneously gripped by passion and hunger.

INGREDIENTS

(Serves 2)

1 tbsp olive oil

250g cubed pancetta (or one packet of bacon)

8 tbsp dry white wine

1 packet fresh spaghetti

6 egg yolks

8 tbsp double cream

60g Parmesan, freshly grated

Freshly ground black pepper, to taste

METHOD

Put a large pan of salted water on to boil.

Heat the olive in a large frying pan. Add the pancetta. When it begins to get crispy, add the wine to the pan and allow it to cook for a few minutes.

Take the pan off the heat and set it aside until everything else is ready.

Once the water has boiled, put in the pasta and cook it according to the instructions on the packet.

Meanwhile, mix together the egg yolks, cream, Parmesan and black pepper.

When the pasta is ready, put the pan with the pancetta back on the hob.

Drain the spaghetti and turn it into the pan with the pancetta.

Whoosh it around a little, so the spaghetti gets evenly covered, then remove the pan from the heat.

Pour over the eggy cheesy mixture and stir it in, ensuring the pasta is fairly evenly coated.

Grind over some more pepper, then serve in huge bowls.

Perfect Bacon Sandwich

There is, I'm reliably informed, a formula for the perfect bacon sandwich. It goes like this: $N = C + \{fb \ (cm) . fb \ (tc)\} + fb \ (Ts) + fc . ta$. Alternatively, you can just follow this recipe for my version.

INGREDIENTS

(Serves 1)

3 rashers of the best possible bacon

Knob of butter

2 slices white bread

METHOD

Fry the bacon in the butter in a frying pan on the hob.

Timing here is crucial – the fat needs to turn slightly golden. Then turn the bacon over and cook the other side. You want the fat to turn deliciously crisp, but for the bacon to remain soft and not at all cardboardy.

Remove the bacon from the frying pan and take a slice of bread and dip one side of it in the pan to mop up the deliciously bacony butter.

Do the same with the other slice, then make up the sandwich.

For those with a scientific bent, the formula in full is:

$N = C + \{fb \ (cm) . fb \ (tc)\} + fb \ (Ts) + fc . ta$. *where*
$N = $ *force in Newtons required to break the cooked bacon*
$fb = $ *function of the bacon type*
$fc = $ *function of the condiment/filling effect*
$Ts = $ *serving temperature*
$tc = $ *cooking time*
$ta = $ *time or duration of application of condiment/filling*
$cm = $ *cooking method*
and $C = $ *Newtons required to break uncooked bacon.*

130

Scrambled Eggs with Thyme

Good scrambled eggs are among my favourite comfort foods, while bad ones are enough to make me cry. They're perfect for midnight feasts as they're sustaining and consoling and making them calls more for care than effort.

INGREDIENTS

(Serves 2)

3 large, fresh organic eggs

30ml double cream

Salt and freshly ground black pepper

1 tsp chopped fresh thyme

15g butter

METHOD

Crack the eggs into a bowl, add the cream, salt and pepper and whisk gently with a fork. Stir in the thyme.

Melt the butter in a small heavy-based pan over a medium heat.

When the butter begins to bubble, pour in the eggs. Let them sit there for about half a minute and then begin to stir gently with a wooden spoon.

Keep stirring off and on until they're almost cooked, but still runny in places.

Remove the pan from the hob and allow the eggs to continue to cook in the pan away from the heat.

After a minute or so, serve the scrambled eggs on hot buttered toast.

Tomato & Pesto Tart

This tart, which I was taught to make by my friend Keith, is just the thing to make if you're whizzing up a midnight feast for a crowd. It tastes delicious, requires almost no effort and makes heaps, so no one will go hungry.

INGREDIENTS

(Makes 12 slices)

Small block of puff pastry

250g ricotta

4 heaped tbsp of pesto

12 tomatoes

METHOD

Pre-heat the oven to 200°C/gas mark 6.

Roll out the pastry to around 40cm x 30cm and 5mm thick.

Line a baking sheet with some baking parchment, place the pastry on top and put a cake cooling rack on top of the pastry as this will stop it from rising too much.

Bake the pastry for around 15 minutes. Turn it over and cook for another 5 minutes. Leave to cool for about 10 minutes.

Mix the ricotta with the pesto and spread the mixture over the pastry. Arrange the tomatoes neatly on the pesto-covered pastry.

Bake in the oven for 10-15 minutes or until the tomatoes become slightly charred.

Delicious hot or cold.

Quesadillas with Salsa

Perfect for the witching hour and – as the ingredients are fairly staple – these make a delicious impromptu midnight snack. If you like your salsa to have a serious kick, simply add another chilli.

INGREDIENTS

(Serves 1)

For the salsa

4 tomatoes

1 spring onion

3 cloves garlic

1 red chilli, de-seeded

2 tbsp coriander

Juice of 2 limes

$^1/_2$ tsp sugar

Salt and pepper

For the filling

30g Cheddar

30g Red Leicester

30g Mozzarella

1 spring onion, chopped

$^1/_2$ red pepper, chopped

Plus

2 flour tortillas

METHOD

Finely chop the tomatoes, onion and garlic. Chop the chilli, removing all the seeds.

Mix all the chopped ingredients in a bowl. Pour over the lime juice and sprinkle the sugar. Season with a little salt and a good grind of pepper and sprinkle over the coriander.

Mix all of the ingredients for the filling together in a bowl. Sprinkle the filling over one of the tortillas and then top with the other, like an ordinary sandwich.

Heat a heavy frying pan on a medium heat. Pop the quesadilla in and cook it for a minute or so on one side before flipping it over and cooking the other side.

The tortilla should brown to a golden colour and the filling should become a glorious, melted goopy mush.

Tip it out of the pan on to a plate and cut into wedges.

Serve with the salsa.

Chocolate Fondue

This is one of those midnight feasts best shared at that delicious, tentative stage when you just begin to fall in love and want to stay up all night talking.

INGREDIENTS

(Serves 2)

200g of the best chocolate you can find (70% cocoa solids)

200ml double cream

Glug of cherry brandy

Strawberries and marshmallows, for dipping

METHOD

I'm presuming you don't have a fondue set, so melt the chocolate in a bowl over a pan of simmering water.

When it's completely melted, remove it from the heat and gradually mix in the cream and cherry brandy.

Take it up to bed in a warm, pretty bowl and eat it as quickly as possible, so it doesn't go cold.

You can use one of those food warmers with candles, but I'm nervous about recommending it as it might be dangerous in bed!

Eton Mess

I can see many reasons why Eton Mess should be kept firmly at the kitchen table – it's messy, the capacity for crumbs is high and it's full of sugar. But it's thrilling to eat in bed and rather romantic spoon-fed to the one you love.

INGREDIENTS

(Serves 2 hungry people)

2 tsp unrefined caster sugar

250g strawberries, hulled and roughly chopped

200ml whipping cream

4 small meringues, broken into small pieces

METHOD

Sprinkle the caster sugar over the strawberries and leave them covered with clingfilm for a while.

Whip the cream until it becomes thick, but be careful not to do it for so long that it becomes stiff.

By now the strawberries should have yielded some of their juice and you can fold them into the cream.

Mix the meringue pieces in with the strawberries and cream.

Serve immediately in bowls or glasses.

Rice Pudding

When I'm feeling vulnerable, I long for the childish comfort of proper rice pudding. Even the smell makes me feel better and the taste takes me back to a time when problems were smaller.

INGREDIENTS

(Serves 2)

75g pudding rice

55g vanilla sugar

300ml full-fat milk

250ml single cream

1 vanilla pod

50g butter

$^1/_2$ tsp nutmeg, freshly grated

METHOD

Pre-heat the oven to 150°C/gas mark 2.

Grease an ovenproof dish with some butter. Rinse the rice under cold water and put it in the dish.

Sprinkle over the sugar, then pour over the milk and cream. Scrape in the seeds from the vanilla pod. Dot the butter over the top and sprinkle with the nutmeg.

Place in the oven for one hour and 15 minutes, stirring after the first 30 minutes.

The cooking times for rice pudding are not an exact science – I've cooked this dish hundreds of times, but somehow the length of time it takes to cook seems to change every time I make it.

If it still seems a bit runny, put it back in for another 10 minutes or so until it's soft and creamy.

Take it out of the oven and leave it for five minutes or so before serving.

Hot Chocolate

Warming and calming, hot chocolate is reminiscent of childhood walks on the beach and somehow drinking a mug in bed insulates you from the outside world. If the mood takes you, a splash of Amaretto will liven things up a bit.

INGREDIENTS

(Serves 2)

5 large squares of good quality milk chocolate

4 tbsp double cream

600ml full-fat milk

METHOD

Melt four squares of chocolate in a saucepan over a low heat. It's really important to do this gently.

With the saucepan still on the heat, mix in the cream, beating quickly with a spoon.

Add the milk slowly, a little at a time, still beating, until you've used it all.

Turn up the heat a fraction and warm the hot chocolate until it's very hot, but not boiling.

Pour the hot chocolate into two mugs and grate the remaining square of chocolate over the top.

Romantic escapes

Hotels and romance go hand in hand. It's almost impossible not to swoon when you contemplate Egyptian cotton sheets, the mini-bar, room service, fluffy towels and everything else that is utterly blissful post check-in.

Vine House
Burnham Market, Norfolk

EVER SINCE I READ *Eloise* when I was around seven, I have wanted to live in a hotel. There's something so cool about the whole experience. Room service, mini bars, high thread-count sheets, properly made beds, fluffy bathrobes, (which would never do at home, but seem divine in a hotel, somehow).

The mini-break is now as important to a love affair as butter has always been to toast. And, of course, no mini-break would be complete without a blissful and leisurely breakfast in bed.

Going away for a weekend, week, or longer can either cement or break a relationship, so it's important to choose where to stay very carefully. When you're in the heady days of a new romance and plan to spend all weekend in bed, then all that really matter are a dreamy bedroom and a great room service menu.

As love moves into a steadier phase, it's rather nice to find somewhere that offers something a little more diverting.

Whether you choose the city or the country, I guess, depends on where you spend most of your time. Living in the wilds of Norfolk, nothing thrills me more than a trip into town. However, my city-based friends long for fresh air, sea and rural views.

Here, I've listed all the places I love to have breakfast in bed and I've talked to my most glamorous friends and have added their suggestions too.

UK – London

The Haymarket
www.firmdale.com

There's something about all the Firmdale hotels in London that just works perfectly. Each one is beautifully designed, the staff are delightful, the food delicious – the best breakfast in London, I think – and they still have smoking rooms, which is such a rarity these days that even non-smokers find it novel. The Haymarket is my current favourite, although that changes on a regular basis and I have been equally passionate about The Charlotte Street Hotel and The Knightsbridge. To be honest, I would be utterly thrilled to be whisked away to any of them. Many of the pictures in this book were taken at the Haymarket.

Miller's Residence
www.millersuk.com

Staying at Miller's is like stepping back in time. *Homes & Gardens* magazine describes it as 'like spending a night in the old curiosity shop' and *The Daily Telegraph* said 'when you first enter you feel as if you've walked onto the set of *La Traviata* in one of its wilder moments'. Not necessarily what you'd expect in Notting Hill. Personally, Miller's would always be my first choice for a night away from home. It is the antithesis of stuffy hotels and you always meet fascinating people when staying there. I also can't think of anywhere I'd rather eat breakfast – you do have to go downstairs and make it yourself, but this, I think, just adds to the charm. Miller's is definitely at its best when its charming owner, Martin, is in residence.

Hazlitt's
www.hazlittshotel.com

Although Hazlitt's is only a few steps away from Soho Square, it's a civilised oasis in the heart of one of the most vibrant parts of London. Adored by writers for its peaceful atmosphere and understated chic, I've never stayed without bumping into at least one author I'm in awe of. The bedrooms are delicious, the bathrooms very sweet and when you step out of the front door you're right in the centre of things.

Blakes
www.blakeshotels.com

Since it opened in the mid 1970s, Blakes has been offering its own brand of discreet decadence. It's blissfully romantic, quirky and conjures up a moment in time when London was at its headiest. This is the perfect hotel for when you're in the first flush of love and are dizzy with desire. If you're planning to spend the entire weekend in bed, then you probably won't find anywhere more opulent to do so. Designed and owned by Anouska Hempel, Blakes is lavish, lovely and luxurious. The scrambled eggs for breakfast are utterly delicious and my only regret is that I've only ever stayed there when alone.

St Martin's Lane
www.stmartinslane.com

Based in the heart of Covent Garden, this is the dream hotel for anyone who adores modern design. It's sleek, minimalist and fun. St Martin's Lane was designed by Philippe Starck, who took his influences from the modern to the baroque. All the bedrooms have floor-to-ceiling windows and a light installation which allows you to 'light your mood', which is huge fun if you're into gadgets. The bathrooms, too, are wonderful. They're huge, white and have the kind of baths that positively encourage social bathing.

The Hoxton Urban Lodge
www.hoxtonhotels.com

Nothing about this hotel says cheap. But with a philosophy of luxury where it matters and budget where it counts this is not only one of the hippest places to stay in London, but also one of the most affordable. Roaring fires, chic cocktails, Aveda products, sumptuous duck-down duvets and luxury sheets, make the Hoxton Urban Lodge a brilliant choice for a romantic night in town.

UK – The country
The Grove, Hertfordshire
www.thegrove.co.uk

This is the perfect place for parents to go for a romantic weekend when they can't find anywhere to leave the kids. I realise this sounds like an utter contradiction, but the Grove really does allow you to spend lots of time with your partner, while the children have a very groovy time of their own. There's a kids' club they have to be dragged out of, as they love it so much, in-room babysitting, so you can enjoy a romantic dinner and lots of interconnecting rooms, so you can enjoy both privacy and the knowledge that the children are safe and having fun.

Fingals, Dartmouth, Devon
www.fingals.co.uk

Quirky, delightful and described by Vic Reeves as 'bonkers', what more could you want from a hotel? Richard Johnston used to run a restaurant of the same name on the Fulham Road and then he stumbled upon a run-down farmhouse in Devon and transformed it into a charming, laid-back retreat. There's also a gorgeous converted barn with two bedrooms and a roll-top bath.

Babington House, Frome, Somerset
www.babingtonhouse.co.uk

The perfect country house weekend with an urban twist. Huge bedrooms, delicious bathrooms stocked full of Cowshed products and with showers that are perfect for two, it's almost impossible not to feel the frisson of romance. It would be a simple case of jolly bad manners not to eat breakfast in bed here and I highly recommend poached eggs

followed by toast and the really scrumptious honey they serve.

Ickworth, Suffolk
www.ickworthhotel.co.uk

There are many reasons to adore Ickworth. The surrounding parkland is perfect for romantic walks, it occupies the east wing of a National Trust House and you can visit the main house during your stay. There's a crèche, babysitting and lots for children to do if you're taking yours with you and there are two great restaurants, one formal and the other informal. There is a mix of modern

Ickworth, Suffolk

Tuddenham Mill

Vine House

The Haymarket

The Haymarket

and traditionally decorated bedrooms in the main house and the Dower House, which is just a short walk from the hotel, houses some apartments. Ickworth is perfect for those into romantic walks and grand architecture. The full English breakfast is well worth staying in bed for.

Feather Down Farms
www.featherdown.co.uk

From Scotland to Cornwall there are enchanting Feather Down Farms. The luxury tents, which are on working, family farms, are lit by chandeliers, have wood-burning stoves, flushing loos and, instead of a fridge, there's a wooden chest packed with ice. Locally sourced food sold in honesty shops and the comfortable beds make Feather Down ideal for romantic camping trips.

Tuddenham Mill, Newmarket, Suffolk
www.tuddenhammill.co.uk

This traditional watermill has undergone a chic renovation and has become the perfect bolthole for couples. The rooms are understated and beautiful and, they don't just welcome dogs, they adore them, which is great for those who love romantic breaks but can't bear to leave Fido at home. Bose sound systems, enormous stone baths and six-foot beds add to the romantic feel. The scrambled duck eggs and smoked salmon are absolutely delicious for breakfast.

Vine House, Burnham Market, Norfolk
www.vinehouseboutiquehotel.co.uk

Vine House – outpost of the hugely successful Hoste Arms in Burnham Market – is attracting an awful lot of attention in its own right. Situated just across the road from the Hoste, it has just seven bedrooms, all of which are beautifully furnished and have great bathrooms. Vine House exudes grown-up glamour. Each evening there's a butler service and guests can use all the Hoste's facilities, including, of course, the restaurant. Breakfast can be either taken at the Hoste or, far more fun in my opinion, you can have a breakfast hamper delivered to you in bed.

Isle of Eriska Hotel, Ledaig, Argyll
www.eriska-hotel.co.uk

What could possibly be more romantic than a private island? Only a private island with an amazing hotel, spa with Ayurvedic-inspired rituals, rooms with hot tubs and delicious food. There are beautiful walks around the island and pebble beaches, so you'll be sure to work up an appetite. The island is linked to the mainland by a small bridge.

Dakota, Forth Bridge, Scotland
www.dakotaforthbridge.co.uk

This is a budget hotel, but it was also named ninth hottest hotel in the world by *Conde Nast Traveller*. It's also been described as 'a little piece of heaven, off junction 27 [of the M1]'. While the location couldn't be described as one of the most romantic, once inside it's blissful. You have everything you'd expect from a luxury hotel, except the huge bill at the end.

Hotel Pelirocco, Brighton
www.hotelpelirocco.co.uk

The Hotel Pelirocco is the original sexy boutique hotel. It describes itself as 'England's most rock 'n' roll hotel'. From music to something a little saucier, there's something for everyone here. The Rough Trade Room, inspired by the record shop, is the perfect boy's room. The Fancy Pants room is designed around, well, knickers actually. There's a 'crazy and kitsch' garden themed room and one designed by Jamie Reid, the man most famous for putting a safety pin through the Queen's lips thus giving punk a visual identity. This is the perfect place to take a Rock Chick or Punk Dad for a memorable romantic break.

Further flung
Soho House, New York, America
www.sohohouseny.com

The Manhattan outpost of Nick Jones' empire is just how you'd imagine it – utterly chic and understated. There are so many reasons to stay here, including the amazing rooftop pool, sumptuous bedrooms, hip Meatpacking District location, groovy

cocktails, amazing food and much, much more. If you're off to New York, you'll remember forever waking up and eating breakfast sprawled across the enormous bed.

Johnson Shore Inn, Hermanville, Prince Edward Island, Nova Scotia, Canada
www.johnsonshoreinn.com

Located on the edge of an island cliff, where every room has stunning views over the ocean, this surely has to be one of the most romantic settings in the world. There's a potato vodka distillery on site. The Smoked Salmon Frittata is delicious for breakfast, but it's rumoured that if you ask very nicely, they'll make you Lobster Eggs Benedict, which is to die for.

Hôtel des Academies et des Arts Paris, France
www.hoteldesacademies.fr

There can be no more romantic city to spend a night than Paris and this hotel is utterly perfect. It can accurately be described as a design hotel, but there's none of the pretension that often goes with the label. Beautiful and cosy, the rooms are small – well this is the Left Bank –but they're cosy rather than claustrophobic. Eat croissants in bed without worrying about the crumbs.

The Tides, Riviera Maya, Mexico
www.tidesrivieramaya.com

The Tides has 29 villas hidden away within

the woods, each one utterly secluded and seriously conducive to romance. If you want to feel as if you're the only two people on earth, then this is the place for you. Gorgeous beaches, an amazing pool, delicious food, four-poster beds and blissful bathrooms, make The Tides perfect for a seriously romantic getaway.

Hotel Metropole, Venice, Italy
www.hotel-venezia-metropole.com
The bedrooms here are seriously elegant and are furnished with amazing period pieces. Perfumed candles and incense burn constantly adding to the heady atmosphere, making it impossible not to feel the odd surge of romantic yearning. The food's amazing and the hotel's resident DJ is considered something of a trend-setter when it comes to chilled-out sounds. Come for the breakfast in bed; stay for everything else.

Dar Wada, Marrakech Medina, Morocco
www.darwarda.com
This tiny hotel has only four bedrooms, so its intimate atmosphere makes it feel far more like a private house. It provides a blissful escape from the hustle and bustle outside and is perfect for candlelit dinners and lazing around in bed all day.

JIA, Shanghai, China
www.jiashanghai.com
Set in a stunning 1920s building, East and West collide to provide a hip, playful, intimate and chic space, which is perfect for those who like adventure but not at the cost of home comforts. Designed by Philippe Starck and with bathrooms crafted from marble and mosaic, JIA Shanghai really is an utterly cool place to hang out.

Silken Gran Hotel Domine Bilbao, Spain
www.hoteles-silken.com
This hotel is perfect for anyone into modern design. Six of the rooms have great views of Bilbao's Guggenheim. It's funky and modern and is a perfect romantic venue for anyone who loves the contemporary. The bedrooms are great and the bathrooms even better, with beautiful Jurassic stone tiles, huge free-standing baths and understated washbowls. Of course, you'll want breakfast in bed, but you'll also want to stroll hand-in-hand around this vibrant city.

101 Hotel, Reykjavík, Iceland
www.101hotel.is
Located in the heart of downtown Reykjavík (101 is the chicest postcode) this hotel offers the perfect place to snuggle up against the cold. Personally, I can't imagine anything more romantic than going in search of the Northern Lights with the one you love and this hotel provides a brilliant place to stop over and marvel at what you have seen.

The Haymarket, London

Making tracks
Getaway playlist

Lazing around in bed together, idly flicking
through the room service menu, requires
a soundtrack that's just the right
mix of laid-back and seductive.

Solid Air
John Martyn

Stuttering (Kiss me again)
Ben's Brother

People Will Say We're in Love
Ray Charles & Betty Carter

Rhiannon
Fleetwood Mac

We're All the Way
Eric Clapton

It Could Happen to You
Miles Davis

Lay Lady Lay
Bob Dylan

Goodnight L.A.
Counting Crows

Volare (Nel Blu Di Pinto Di Blu)
Dean Martin

Jolene
The White Stripes

Shopping

Planning, decorating and furnishing a bedroom is enormous fun and is made so much easier with a few inside secrets. I've plundered my address books and those of a number of interiors gurus and here's what we've come up with.

WHEREAS ONCE, not so long ago, shopping was seen as sport or pastime, rather like knitting or football, it now seems to be taking its rightful place in the world. This, I think, is a very good thing.

Consumerism and the one-upmanship of materialism has definitely had its day. Now that we've begun buying things for the right reasons, nice things will once again feel like a huge treat rather than a pressure.

One of the brilliant side effects of all of this is that the things we surround ourselves with will take on much more significance and we'll choose more carefully and wisely. I can't think of anywhere that this is better news, than in the bedroom, as it should be somewhere comforting and cosseting and should not be shaped by the vagaries of fashion.

You need to ensure you create a room that suits your personality. If you're a rock chick, then having a pretty, girlie room, upholstered in fabric dotted in tea roses, will eventually drive you quite bonkers. I know this sounds obvious, but you'd be surprised how many people fall into the trap of designing a room that simply doesn't suit them.

I'm hugely fond of sample pots of paint and swatches of fabric as I think you need to live with something for a few days before you can really make up your mind if it's you or not. The best bedrooms in my opinion are those that have an eclectic feel and have evolved over time. I love walking into a room that has a mix of interesting things picked up from all over the world. It's great to see the personal history of the room's owner stamped all over it. It does help, though, to know where to shop for the basics.

Beds

When it comes to bedrooms, the bed is a good place to start. Bed is a place you'll be spending lots of time, so you should take a long time researching and choosing the one that is perfect for you. I can't stress enough that it's a really good idea to invest a decent amount of money in your bed, even if it means cutting corners elsewhere in the bedroom budget.

If you've had a windfall, funds are limitless or you've decided to invest heavily in a bed, then it's unlikely you'll find one better than those made by Savoir (www.savoirbeds.co.uk). The famous No. 2 bed is quite the most blissful I've ever slept in. It was commissioned in the early 1900s by the Savoy Hotel and can be made to any size or shape you like.

Another very good option if you're looking for a luxury bed is And so to Bed (www.andsotobed.co.uk). The company has a huge range of unbelievably gorgeous

bedsteads and deliciously comfortable mattresses. If you're looking for a wide range of bed options, are unsure what you'd like to spend, or are on a tight budget, then a department store is a good place to go bed shopping. John Lewis (www.johnlewis.com) has a good selection and very helpful and knowledgeable staff. Also, as they have stores all over the country, you don't have to travel miles to find one.

Fabrics and wall coverings

The colour you use in your bedroom really sets the tone and mood. It's a good idea to pick two or three colours that work well together as your main colours and build from there.

Colour really can affect your mood, so it's important to choose well, particularly when it comes to the bedroom. Patterns, too, are important – too busy and you'll never get to sleep, too bland and you'll be driven to distraction. If you're going to go for patterned wallpaper or fabric, then you need to make sure the pattern is one you will adore for years to come and not simply a passing fancy.

When it comes to fabrics, Cabbages and Roses (www.cabbagesandroses.com) is one of my favourite companies. Everything they sell is quintessentially English, beautiful and timeless and they also sell readymade

cushions and the odd throw.

Designers Guild (www.designersguild.com) is a great option for fabrics and wallpaper. Founder and creative director Tricia Guild has a knack for mixing unusual colours and prints and somehow creating something that is both sumptuous and optimistic.

If you like fabrics to be warm and opulent, then it's well worth checking out the range at Colony Fabrics (www.colonyfabrics.com) as the colours and patterns are rich and warm.

GP & J Baker (www.gpjbaker.com) has been producing beautiful prints and weaves for well over 100 years and has one of the largest and most exciting textile archives in the world. If you have a fabric fetish, this is definitely one company you should be getting to know.

George Smith (www.georgesmith.co.uk) is perhaps best known for furniture, but the company does have a very pleasing range of fabrics too and shouldn't be overlooked when shopping for the bedroom.

Ecocentric (www.ecocentric.co.uk) has a lovely range of wallpapers on its website, as well as lots of other interesting bedroom items, including cushions, blankets and throws. As well as being very lovely indeed, all the products stocked on this website are also ethical and eco-friendly.

Linen

The linen you choose for your bed will have a serious bearing on the quality of sleep you achieve, which is why it pays to invest a little bit more in your bed linen and then make sure you care for it brilliantly.

A brilliant one-stop shop for everything you need for your bed is The White Company (www.thewhitecompany.com). It has everything from mattress covers through to throws and all at reasonable prices.

The Monogrammed Linen Shop (www.mono-grammedlinenshop.com) has a blissful range of truly beautiful bedroom luxuries. Its cashmere blankets are to die for, as is the linen for which the company is famous.

Really good for old-fashioned styles, the fabulous Cologne & Cotton (www.cologneandcotton.com) also do a really good line in stripy linen, which I absolutely love.

Paint

I love bedrooms with painted walls. I think for everybody there is a colour out there that is 'the one'. This is a recent discovery for me as I've flirted with many hues throughout the years, have had fun with a lots of shades and have enjoyed colours immensely.

But, it wasn't until I fell head over heels with the colour that my bedroom is painted that I realised once you get serious about a colour, you really know it. The colour that I fell in love with is called Mercury and is by Fired Earth. It is quite the most exquisite colour I have ever seen and has transformed my bedroom from an ordinary primrose Georgian room into the bedroom I have dreamed of all my life.

Fired Earth (www.firedearth.com) paint offers brilliant coverage, a serious range of neutrals (they firmly believe there's no such colour as white) and some truly striking colours. There are also a few colours in the Designers Guild (www.designersguild.com) range that I believe it would be tricky to live without.

Sleepwear

What you wear in bed is jolly important – even if there's no one there to see you. My favourite pyjamas are those from Shanghai Tang (www.shanghaitang.com). They're beautifully cut, made from divine fabrics and make you look elegant and skinny even on a fat day. If you need something a little more seductive than buttoned-to-the-top pyjamas, then nightwear doesn't come much sexier than the silk nightdresses from The Monogrammed Linen Shop (www.monogrammedlinenshop.com). I defy any man to be able to resist a girl decked out in one of these.

Get the look
Shop from the book

I think each time a man puts on a pair of pyjamas he should try to channel James Stewart in *Rear Window* and therefore believe very strongly in pyjamas from companies such as Brooks Brothers (www.brooksbrothers.com). Their pale blue ones with dark blue piping make me swoon a little.

The Pyjama Room (www.pyjamaroom.com) has a great range of pyjamas, dressing gowns, nightdresses and things to slouch around in at home that score highly on the glamour scale. It's a good place for men to shop for presents, as everything is gorgeous.

Some of my favourite nightwear comes from Cath Kidston (www.cathkidston.co.uk). It's pretty, easy to wear and is utterly cosy in a deliciously retro way. While it's definitely not sleepwear to seduce in, it's utterly divine for duvet days. My long flowery nightdress, cashmere cardigan and bedsocks always feel rather chic in a 1940s sort of way.

Details of some of the bedroom accessories featured in Breakfast in Bed.

Green silk nightdress and cashmere throw **(p23) by the Monogrammed Linen Shop** (www.monogrammedlinenshop.com)

Peter Rabbit breakfast set **(p72-73, 75 & p86) by Wedgwood** (www.wedgwood.com)

Scrabble® board game **(p76) by Hasbro** (www.hasbro.com)

Shoes **(p94) by Christian Louboutin** (www.christianlouboutin.com) **and Converse** (www.converse.com)

Long-cabled hand-knitted bed socks **(p110) by Toast** (www.toast.co.uk)

Dreams and Thoughts notebooks **and correspondence cards (p114) by Smythson** (www.smythson.com)

Pink pyjamas **(p114 & 160) by Shanghai Tang** (www.shanghaitang.com)

Heart-shaped silver toast rack **(p121) by Fortnum & Mason** (www.fortnumandmason.com)

Butter dish **(p121) by Emma Bridgewater** (www.emmabridgewater.co.uk)

Acknowledgements

Writing any book is a huge team effort and I'd like to thank the following for making the whole thing possible.

MY VERY LOVELY commissioning editor, Meg Avent, who had the brilliant idea for this book and then the less brilliant idea of asking me to write it.

Jon Croft, my publisher at Absolute Press, who was – as always – urbane, charming and huge fun.

Matt Inwood, whose good cop-bad cop routine on missed deadlines was hugely funny and well worth missing an important date or two for.

Antony Topping; could anyone have a nicer agent?

The fabulous Elizabeth of Mar, who is quite the sunniest, loveliest person I have ever worked with and who is not only brilliant at publicity, but is also a kind and true friend.

Tim, who designed this book utterly beautifully and provided beautiful images, support and encouragement. I'm extremely lucky to have such huge talent so close.

Lisa Barber, for the great food photography, and Trish Hilferty for styling the images so chicly.

Delaval Astley, Keith Wyatt and everyone at Back to the Garden for access to amazing ingredients and knowledge, and Jon Hadley, for literally keeping my house in order.

A book is never written in a vacuum and real life goes on as one bashes away at the Mac keyboard.

While writing this, life for me has been turbulent to say the least and full of loss and sadness. I truly mean it when I say I don't know how I would have got through it without the help of my wonderful friends, among them Raffaella Barker, Jenny Heller, William Higham, Isobel Rose, Miv Watts, Richard Scarre, John Dabb and Lizzie Falconer.

Thank you, too, to my lovely new friend, Simon. They say people come into your life for a reason, a season or a lifetime and I sincerely hope he will stick around.

I would also like to thank Elbow for their fabulous album *Seldom Seen Kid*, which provided the soundtrack for this project and which I have listened to on a loop during the entire writing process.

And finally, as ever, a huge thank you to my adorable children for their patience, recipe testing skills and utter gorgeousness.

Laura James

Norfolk, 2008

157

LAURA JAMES is an author, columnist and journalist. She writes on fashion, food, trends, interiors, beauty, etiquette and modern life for many newspapers and magazines. *Breakfast in Bed* is her seventh book. Laura is also Brand Ambassador for Aga.

When not sitting by her own Aga, frantically bashing out copy, Laura is most usually found lazing in bed, propped up on pillows, munching delicious food and listening to loud music.

Laura lives in bohemian chaos in north Norfolk, and has far too many children and pets, including a soppy Labrador, a kleptomaniac dachshund, two Bengal cats and a tortoise.